The Remedial Writing Teacher's Handbook

Vicki L. Hackett and
Paul C. Dalmas

WALCH PUBLISHING

User's Guide
to
Walch Reproducible Books

As part of our general effort to provide educational materials which are as practical and economical as possible, we have designated this publication a "reproducible book." The designation means that purchase of the book includes purchase of the right to limited reproduction of all pages on which this symbol appears:

Here is the basic Walch policy: We grant to individual purchasers of this book the right to make sufficient copies of reproducible pages for use by all students of a single teacher. This permission is limited to a single teacher, and does not apply to entire schools or school systems, so institutions purchasing the book should pass the permission on to a single teacher. Copying of the book or its parts for resale is prohibited.

Any questions regarding this policy or requests to purchase further reproduction rights should be addressed to:

Permissions Editor
J. Weston Walch, Publisher
321 Valley Street • P. O. Box 658
Portland, Maine 04104-0658

---

1   2   3   4   5   6   7   8   9   10

ISBN 0-8251-2844-7

Copyright © 1982, 1996
J. Weston Walch, Publisher
P.O. Box 658 • Portland, Maine 04104-0658

Printed in the United States of America

Contents

PART TWO. *Writing Projects*

PART THREE. Other Competencies

Acknowledgments

Friss, Dick, *Writing Class: Teacher and Students Writing Together,* Bay Area Writing Project, University of California, Berkeley, California, 1981. (Curriculum Publication No. 11, 5635 Tolman Hall, University of California, Berkeley, CA 94720.)

Hartley, William G., and Gary L. Shumway. *An Oral History Primer,* Primer Publications, Salt Lake City, Utah, 1973. (P.O. Box 11894, Salt Lake City, UT 84147.)

Pat Boyd, English Teacher, Mount Diablo School District, Concord, California.

Jo Fyfe, Consultant, Bay Area Writing Project, University of California, Berkeley.

Mary K. Healy, Consultant, Bay Area Writing Project, University of California, Berkeley.

Chris Honoré, Consultant, Bay Area Writing Project, University of California, Berkeley.

Marilyn Iversen, English Teacher, Mount Diablo School District, Concord, California.

Joan R. MacLellan, English Teacher, Mount Diablo School District, Concord, California.

Michael Rodriguez, District Coordinator of English Teachers, Mount Diablo School District, Concord, California.

Mary Ann Smith, Consultant, Bay Area Writing Project, University of California, Berkeley.

Catherine Schengel Townsley, Consultant, Bay Area Writing Project, University of California, Berkeley.

Bob Skapura, Librarian, Mount Diablo School District, Concord, California.

Bill Thomas, English Department Chairman, Mount Diablo School District, Concord, California.

Introduction

The Remedial Writing Teacher's Handbook is designed to help you prepare your high school students to pass a competency test in writing. Competency tests, or basic skills tests, are now required for graduation by many states.

With the advent of these tests, administered either by the state or the local school district, many students are realizing the seriousness of their situation. The poor writers can and may be assessed at any grade level. However, the crucial stage for most of these remedial writers is the tenth through twelfth grades, the period during which most of them must pass the competency test in writing. During this time, motivation to pass and thus to improve basic writing skills, is at its height—especially for those students who have once failed the writing test. It is for this particular period in the students' academic career that *The Remedial Writing Teacher's Handbook* is intended.

Another trend in education today is the reduction of staff due to declining enrollment and budget cutbacks at state and local levels. It is an unfortunate reality that good teachers are often assigned to instruct in areas outside their special fields in order to fit the school's particular program. Therefore, in writing this book we have had in mind not only experienced English teachers but also those who find themselves teaching remedial composition for the first time.

In our research, we have found that states and districts take various approaches to the testing of writing competencies. Some tests present several choices of one type of writing, such as a business letter, and ask the student to indicate which is in the correct form. Some tests require the student to correct the errors in a particular piece of writing, such as a paragraph. Some require the student to write different types of compositions, such as a narrative paragraph, a résumé, a business letter, and an essay. Some tests are a combination of two or three of these approaches. This book is designed to help your students actually learn to write in various

forms. Your students will be able to recognize a good piece of writing and to correct errors if they must. But basically they will be able to write, meeting minimal competency standards, regardless of the test they face.

Because the duration of remedial writing classes varies (indeed, such classes do not even exist in many areas), *The Remedial Writing Teacher's Handbook* is organized so that you and your students can work on those skills that must be mastered first. A glance at the table of contents will provide you with appropriate curriculum choices for the grading period preceding the testing.

We do not believe that the teaching of writing should end when your students pass the writing competency test. Therefore, additional writing instruction is provided to enable your struggling remedial writers to continue practicing their recently developed skills. The writing experiences we suggest are parallels of assignments the better writers in your school are doing, from personal narrative to actual research papers, but on a level appropriate—and with the instruction necessary— for the remedial writer.

The Remedial Writing Teacher's Handbook is divided into three major sections. Part One focuses on the sentence, the paragraph, the essay, and the personal and business letters. Part Two presents several writing projects and approaches for students who have completed Part One and continue to develop in a composition class. Part Three is devoted to other competency skills, ranging from the completing of applications and forms to résumé writing, examined in various competency tests across the country. The worksheets and exercises at the end of each chapter, designated by the copyright line at the bottom of the page, may be duplicated and handed out to your students.

We wish to express our appreciation to the many educators who contributed their knowledge to the development of this curriculum for the remedial writer.

PART ONE

Basic Writing Competencies

CHAPTER 1

Class Organization and Strategies

Students in a remedial composition program are special people. Chances are that they have spent many school hours not understanding, not listening, and not producing. Once they have been identified as people who do not do well in school, they have probably spent their time not being challenged and not caring about success. Faced with passing a competency exam in order to graduate from high school, such students may for the first time be motivated to improve their writing. In our experience, this motivation can be practically a guarantee of a successful and worthwhile year in a course designed to remedy deficient writing. What follows are some general strategies and organizational ideas that have worked for us and that we think may be useful to others.

Student Folders and Weekly Assignment Sheets

Clearly, students who have not had much success need to experience a sense of accomplishment. Two simple techniques to assure this are student work folders and weekly assignment sheets.

Keeping all of a student's work in a manila folder in the classroom is an excellent way of reminding the student of just how much he or she has accomplished. As the folder grows, confidence in writing usually does also. The mere bulk of the folder is evidence to the student of an ability to write. In addition, the folder provides as detailed a record as possible of individual progress. The student can see how his or her writing has grown in quality as well as quantity during the semester.

Another useful tool is the weekly assignment sheet, an example of which is provided on page 5. This sheet is kept in the work folder and records attendance, assignments, and a weekly grade. Each day, the student records attendance and assigned

responsibility for the class period, whether it is writing, reading, listening to a lesson, or participating in a discussion. At the end of each week, the sheets are collected and students are assigned daily points and a weekly grade. Students are always aware of how they are doing and whether they have missed any work. They can also be held accountable for missed work and be assigned a due date for it. The weekly grades may be integrated into the course grade.

Both the folder and the assignment sheet give the course a sense of continuity that students cannot ignore. They know they have been working and learning. They are aware of their successes.

Board Work, Exercises, and Computer Writing

The course we are describing has a very practical goal: passing a competency exam in writing. Because of this show-me-how-to-pass character of the course, we feel it is necessary in the classroom to demonstrate as well as explain the process of writing. The constant use of the board (or the overhead projector) is essential to accomplish this. Explaining, brainstorming, and composing writing samples with the class are all made easier when ideas are jotted on the board so that students can see writing is an activity they can easily imitate.

Individual exercises enable classwork to be tailored to the students' needs. In fact, the best exercises are often based on writing that students have produced. Such assignments provide firsthand examples of the specific virtues and problems of the class members. If practical, allow students to write at a computer. With a word processor, they can more easily revise, rearrange sentences and paragraphs, and correct spelling errors.

Writing with the Students

We strongly believe you should write with your students as often as possible. Because remedial writing students demand so much help as they write, it is extremely difficult for a teacher to sit down and write an assignment along with students during a class period. Despite this, we urge you to write in class a minimum of once a month. In this way, students can begin to see that writing is an activity that real people actually participate in and derive satisfaction from, rather than a torture that students are forced to suffer through. If you then share your writing with the class, especially if the subject matter reveals something of your life beyond the classroom, the nature of your student–teacher relationship may change. Students begin to see you differently, and the writing process will become a challenging but rewarding activity that you and your class face together.

An extremely helpful resource in this area is Dick Friss's book *Writing Class: Teacher and Students Writing Together*, published by the Bay Area Writing Project at the University of California at Berkeley. The book traces the growth of a single student writer through a semester in a remedial writing class and shows how teacher writing was a help.

The Workshop Approach

We also highly recommend the use of the writers' workshop. In this strategy, after a rough draft of an assignment has been completed, small groups of writers read each other's papers and evaluate them according to specific guidelines. An example of the sheet we use for student comments is provided on page 6. The process is more fully described in the writing units later in this book and in Friss's book. Your participation in these workshops, occasionally if not every time they occur, can do wonders for your credibility as a teacher, a writer, and a person. When students realize that they can actually make suggestions to their teacher, they are in for a tremendous ego boost.

Writing in Subject Areas Outside English

English is obviously not the only class in which high school students are required to write. History, civics, science, and other subject areas make constant writing demands upon students regardless of their skill, and in all but the rarest cases these assignments are made with no instruction in writing.

Remedial writers are thus often left floundering with seemingly impossible assignments that they complete minimally, if at all.

Yet the remedial writing teacher is in an excellent position to take advantage of this unfortunate situation by being available to help students with their written work for other classes. By expressing this desire to help and by setting aside class time on a regular basis for work from other courses, you will be providing a service about which your students are both enthusiastic and grateful. Students receive the help they feel they need, and what they have learned in their writing class carries over into other subjects. We have also found teachers in other disciplines anxious to have us help their students and more than willing to discuss their assignments and expectations.

Working with Library Materials

A writing class in preparation for a competency exam will be the last English class for many of our students, and therefore the last chance for them to discover what libraries have to offer. Several of the projects we have designed for the second semester of the course demonstrate the richness of the library as a resource, not only during the high school years but also throughout life.

Language Problems

Any course in remedial composition must somehow confront the problems of vocabulary, spelling, mechanics, and usage. We feel that these skills are most effectively developed by means other than setting aside weeks of time solely for language study. Such units usually seem interminable to students and tend to isolate the importance of the skills studied; students are concerned for a limited period of time, after which the skills are forgotten.

We prefer several strategies that continue through the year. Weekly vocabulary or spelling tests, possibly using words from student writing or reading assignments, are the most obvious way to solve part of the problem. Some teachers also have students keep individual lists of words they have misspelled in their writing. These words must be mastered by the end of the grading period. Setting aside one day a week for work on usage and mechanics is also a successful method, especially if the week's lesson is related to the current writing assignment. For instance, Chapter 10 of this book includes an exercise in paragraphing and punctuating conversation (pages 95–96). Finally, we should mention the success we have had in having students catch their own mistakes by reading their writing aloud to us. Students will be surprised to find that a large number of language errors are the result of not proofreading carefully.

Independent Reading

Reading skills and writing skills are inextricably bound together. Because of this, we suggest that remedial writing classes include a program of independent reading—guided, encouraged, and evaluated by the teacher. You can do this by setting aside one period each week when students may read books of their own choosing. Student accountability is an integral part of a reading program, and good use of class reading time is facilitated by a chart on which students record the reading they have accomplished in class. (A copy of such a chart is provided on page 7.) On it, students must indicate what and how much they have read and make a brief comment in the form of a summary or a reaction. If kept in the student work folder, this record also provides a convenient way to keep track of the student's reading.

You may also want to establish a requirement for the amount of reading to be completed during each grading period. When a student finishes a book, a further check on his or her reading may be provided in the form of a written report, an oral presentation to the class, or a brief teacher conference. Independent reading can be made even more useful by paralleling it whenever possible with writing projects assigned in class. The reading of a biography may, for example, be assigned while the class works on the biographical sketch unit described in Chapter 9.

Oral Participation

Because many reluctant writers are much more successful as speakers, we feel oral activity is an important part of any remedial writing class. These activities may take a variety of forms; the important thing is to encourage students to use language constructively to help their writing. We have already mentioned the success we have had in getting students to recognize their errors in language by reading their rough drafts aloud while we work with them one-to-one. Interviews to gather material for writing are another way of using talk to help writing. This is discussed further in Chapter 9. Brainstorming ideas in a freewheeling class discussion can be an exciting way to start an assignment. As students gain confidence and become more at home in the class, formal presentations on independent reading or a demonstration such as that described in Chapter 6 on giving and following instructions can be tried. All of these activities use processes akin to writing and can only serve to increase student success in writing.

These strategies and organizational ideas are an enumeration of what we expect from our students and of what they can expect from us. It is a statement of what we feel a remedial writing class should be—a place where students are held accountable, yet are comfortable about what they are doing. The remainder of the book is devoted to ideas we have invented ourselves and gathered from others to help students write more effectively.

Name _____

Date _____

Weekly Assignment Sheet

Each day is worth 20 points   **Total Points** _____   **Grade** _____

Monday Present _____ Tardy _____ Not Present _____ Points _____	Assignment:
Tuesday Present _____ Tardy _____ Not Present _____ Points _____	Assignment:
Wednesday Present _____ Tardy _____ Not Present _____ Points _____	Assignment:
Thursday Present _____ Tardy _____ Not Present _____ Points _____	Assignment:
Friday Present _____ Tardy _____ Not Present _____ Points _____	Assignment:

Writing Workshop Sheet

Assignment _____

First Evaluator _____

Comments:

Second Evaluator _____

Comments:

Third Evaluator _____

Comments:

Fourth Evaluator _____

Comments:

Name _____

Date _____

Outside Reading Record

Grading Period _____

Date: Book Title: Read from page _____ to page _____ . Comments:	Date: Book Title: Read from page _____ to page _____ . Comments:
Date: Book Title: Read from page _____ to page _____ . Comments:	Date: Book Title: Read from page _____ to page _____ . Comments:
Date: Book Title: Read from page _____ to page _____ . Comments:	Date: Book Title: Read from page _____ to page _____ . Comments:
Date: Book Title: Read from page _____ to page _____ . Comments:	Date: Book Title: Read from page _____ to page _____ . Comments:
Date: Book Title: Read from page _____ to page _____ . Comments:	Date: Book Title: Read from page _____ to page _____ . Comments:

Chapter 2

The Sentence

Sentence-Combining Unit

One of the most obvious problems of most students entering a remedial writing class is the short, choppy sentences they use when they write. This unit is designed around a series of exercises that will help such students begin to move toward a more mature use of syntax. The unit is divided into three phases. Students first learn a process called sentence combining which forces them to write longer, more sophisticated sentences. Next, students continue to combine sentences but also do short writing assignments that invite them to use the new sentence forms they have learned. Finally they do a long, polished paper in which they may demonstrate all they have learned.

The unit, as written, will last about two weeks if followed day by day. However, with the exception of the long paper at the end, the lessons are independent and may be given at the rate of one a week for several weeks, possibly during the time when the paragraph and essay-writing units are covered. The unit requires no special materials and should be followed by the unit on sentence modeling.

Lesson One. Give students a general outline of the unit and discuss its goals. Then pass out the sentence-combining worksheets for Lesson One (A) and Lesson One (B), pages 12–13. Explain that Lesson One (A) consists of twenty short sentences, each containing a single piece of information, and demonstrate this by reading the twenty sentences aloud. Of course, students should never write sentences like this, since mature sentences contain many bits of information. Hence, the exercise asks students to combine the twenty short sentences into six longer ones, one for each group of sentences on the page (one for sentences 1 to 4, one for 5 and 6, one for 7 to 9, and so on). Read the combined example in the box on page 12. Point out the way several short sentences have been combined into each longer one.

The entire class will now do a second combination of the same twenty sentences. Ask the class for an alternate combination of sentences 1 to 4 and write it on the chalkboard. Go through the remaining groups of sentences, using student suggestions and being sure to include all the information each group contains. The class should copy down the new combination as you proceed. A second combination of the twenty sentences might look like this:

> Sitting on a table in the middle of the room is a colorful Monopoly™ board. Small objects cover the board. Some objects are tiny green buildings. Others are yellow and orange cardboard cards. Play money made of paper is also on the table. It is arranged in one large pile and one small pile.

Students are now ready to do their first combination on their own. Go over the worksheet instructions for Lesson One (B). Read the entire set of sentences aloud. This reading is important, though tedious, since it gives the class an idea of all the information that must be covered before work begins. Let the class start work, and be available to make suggestions and to help students who have difficulty. When all the students have finished (in about fifteen minutes), have several read their work aloud, or read it aloud for them. Point out different successful approaches as they appear. If time allows, have the class do the same set of sentences a second time and again read some of the attempts aloud. Collect the written work for credit.

Lesson Two. Begin class by reviewing the goals of the unit then pass out the worksheet for Lesson Two (page 14). Read the first set of sentences aloud and do them on the chalkboard according to student suggestions, as in Lesson One. Then have the class do the same set of fifteen sentences individually, but combining them in a different way. Assist those who need help and be sure several papers are read aloud and different approaches noted. Students may now do the second set of combinations on their own after you have read the sentences aloud. When the class has finished, read aloud some of the more unusual and successful papers. Collect the written work for credit.

Lesson Three. Now that students have done some combining, they are ready to work without the crutch of already-grouped sentences. Additionally, they will now do only a single combination for each lesson before going on to a short writing assignment in which they are encouraged to write sentences similar to those they have combined. Pass out the Lesson Three worksheet (page 15) and read the sentences to be combined. Point out that these sentences may sometimes be easily combined by using several descriptive details in a series in the same sentence. For example: **Isabel had huge, deep, dark eyes that always smiled and long, glossy braids**. Also mention that it is not necessary to use details in the same order as they appear in the exercise. Isabel's braids might be mentioned before her eyes. Let the class work on the combination, but do not allow them to go on to the writing assignment. After the class has completed the worksheet, read several combinations aloud and discuss their virtues. Then read the writing assignment and let the class work on it for the remainder of the period. At the end of the period, read aloud some of the descriptions of friends and collect the written work for credit.

Lesson Four. Pass out the sentence-combining worksheet for Lesson Four (page 16). For the first time, students are asked in the instructions to minimize the number of sentences in their combinations, thereby forcing more information into each sentence and increasing the complexity of the syntax. Read aloud the directions and the sentences to be combined, and make some suggestions for combining. Mention that everyone should be able to combine the short sentences into no more than six or seven longer ones. Let the class proceed with the exercise, but do not let them start the writing assignment until you have read aloud some examples of the combinations. Then have the class work on the writing assignment for the rest of the period. Collect the written work for credit.

Lesson Five. Proceed with Lesson Five (page 17) as you did with Lessons Three and Four. However, in reading the sentences to be combined before students start work, point out that several sentences in this exercise may be easily combined by using a series of **-ing** words (participles) in a longer sentence. For example: **I spent long hours with my**

bike, riding in my neighborhood, exploring other parts of town, and seeking new, exciting adventures**. As the students begin to work, be available as usual and read aloud good examples of combinations and of the writing assignment. Collect the written work for credit.

Lesson Six. This is similar to earlier lessons. Pass out the worksheet for Lesson Six (page 18), and again point out the efficiency of **-ing** words or combining details while going over the exercise. Be available to help with suggestions, read good work aloud, and collect written work for credit.

Lesson Seven. This lesson worksheet for Lesson Seven (page 19) is the last the class will do before embarking on the major paper for the unit, so remind students that this is their last chance to practice each of the skills they have been working on. Otherwise, treat this lesson like the earlier ones, reading examples, helping whenever possible, and collecting written work for credit.

Lesson Eight. Today students will begin the major assignment in which they will demonstrate their new sentence-writing skills. Pass out the Lesson Eight worksheet (page 20) and slowly go over the assignment. As you read, give students ideas for the kinds of people and activities that could be shown in each topic. Ask them to select their topics, then go over the prewriting exercise on the bottom of the worksheet. This chart is designed to help students brainstorm ideas for the rough draft. Their papers may describe a group in general (indeed, this would be a good way to begin), but they should also concentrate on at least four people in detail, doing several long sentences on each. Therefore, they will want to think about each of the four people and jot down some notes before they start to write. The chart is for these notes. Allow the class to start their prewriting charts and, if time allows, their rough drafts. The charts should be kept to use as they write and to turn in later.

Lesson Nine. Using their prewriting charts from the Lesson Eight worksheet, students continue their rough drafts, which are due at the end of the period. Be available to help as needed.

Lesson Ten. Today students will help one another rework their rough drafts in a writing workshop before beginning their final drafts. If this is the class's first writing workshop, explain that this is a process they will be using in one form or another throughout the course. Write the following instructions on the chalkboard and go over them:

A. Exchange papers with another student and do the following:

1. Read the paper carefully.

2. Underline any group of sentences that would be better if combined.

3. Circle similar beginnings of sentences.

4. Put a rectangle around any errors you find in spelling or punctuation.

5. Put a star next to the sentence you think is the best in the paper.

6. Sign the paper at the bottom of the last page.

7. Discuss the marks you have made with the writer of the paper.

B. Repeat steps 1 to 7 with a second student.

C. Check anything you are unsure about with the teacher.

D. Start rewriting your paper. Use suggestions that seem good to you.

Circulate as the students work and be available to help as problems arise.

Lesson Eleven. Students finish rewriting their papers, turning in their final drafts, rough drafts, and prewriting charts at the end of the period. Read and grade the papers out of class and note each student's degree of growth in mastering the material.

Follow-up Activities

1. Continue to emphasize combining short sentences into longer ones in comments on rough and final drafts of papers throughout the course.

2. Some teachers have had success asking students to expand pieces of their writing into sentence-combining exercises. Students then exchange their exercises with other students who recombine the exercises into new pieces of writing.

3. For teachers who find combining exercises especially valuable for their students, we recommend William Strong's *Sentence Combining: A Composing Book*, published by Random House.

Sentence-Modeling Unit

By presenting your class with sentences of varied structures to model, you can help your students develop the confidence they need to try new structures on their own.

Worksheets. Use Worksheets 11–20 at various times during the remediation process, not all at once. Each worksheet is self-explanatory and self-contained, including complete directions and a model. Before assigning any worksheets, be sure your students are familiar with the Introduction to Sentence Modeling (page 21).

The sentences on the worksheets were selected from high-interest, easy-to-read books for young people. The sentences and the book titles and authors might lead some students to the library in search of a book to read. An annotated bibliography follows, in case students ask you about the books.

Sentence-Modeling Bibliography

Bless the Beasts and Children. Glendon Swarthout.
Six boys ranging in ages from twelve to fourteen, disgusting failures in the eyes of their camp society, create their own cabin. Here they cry and "bump" and help one another. Finally they are driven to the limit of endurance by Cotton, their leader, so they can free the buffalo the hunters are trying to kill at the reserve. Emotionally involving book that presents flashback explanations of the six boys' problems. (Doubleday, 1970)

The Chocolate War. Robert Cormier.
A school gang and a ruthless principal try to force a freshman to raise money for the school by selling candy. The story is about gangs and power, and about a teenager facing a confusing maturity. (Dell, 1975)

Fawn. Robert Newton Peck.
The son of a French father and a Mohawk mother, Fawn does not choose sides during the bloody summer of 1758 when Fort Ticonderoga is attacked. He knows that the land is neither French nor British, but his—American. (Dell, 1977)

Gentlehands. M.E. Kerr.
His family objects to sixteen-year-old Buddy's falling in love with an upper-class girl. Only Buddy's mysterious grandfather offers the couple understanding, but their lives are shattered when the grandfather is accused of being a Nazi war criminal. (Harper and Row, 1978)

I Am the Cheese. Robert Cormier.
A gripping tale of government corruption, espionage, and counterespionage is woven skillfully together. Adam Farmer's story of fleeing on bicycle to find his father is woven with the story of his father's testimony about a criminal organization and the family's relocation and reidentification. The ending is a surprise and the suspense is superb. (Dell, 1978)

I Heard the Owl Call My Name. Margaret Craven.
Mark Brian, a young Anglican priest who has only three years to live, is sent to Kingcome, a remote Indian parish in British Columbia. Living simply, close to nature, Mark is able to accept death, even his own, as a part of the circle of life. (Dell, 1974)

The Incredible Journey. Sheila Burnford.
Eager to return to their master, a young Labrador retriever, a Siamese cat, and an old bull terrier set out on a 250-mile journey through the Canadian wilderness and encounter starvation, exposure, a hungry bobcat, and a bear. (Little, Brown, 1960)

Joy in the Morning. Betty Smith.
The time is 1927 when Carl Brown and Annie McGairy of Brooklyn meet and fall in love. Through the very lean years of college for Carl, babies for Annie, parental opposition, and lack of education for Annie, their marriage struggles to survive and makes it. (Harper and Row, 1976)

Rumors of Peace. Ella Leffland.
Eleven-year-old Suse Hansen lives in a small Bay Area northern California town in 1941. With the bombing of Pearl Harbor, panic and confusion come into her life. Her maturing takes place during a troubled time in our history. (Harper and Row, 1976)

Say Hello to the Hit Man. Jay Bennett.
Fred Morgan's father is involved in big-time crime, so Fred changes his name and becomes a serious university student. But he can't get rid of family ties, and when he receives a threatening phone call, he knows his life is in danger. (Delacorte, 1976)

Something Left to Lose. Robin F. Brancato.
A group of girls entering high school experience problems with boys, parents, and class elections. Rebbie has difficulty coping with her alcoholic mother, who is in and out of institutions. She involves her best friend, Jane Ann, in actions that are against the rules of her family and against the law. (Alfred A. Knopf, 1976)

Steffie Can't Come Out to Play. Fran Arrick.
Alone and scared in New York City, fourteen-year-old Steffie unwittingly finds herself involved with a pimp and becomes one of the city's young prostitutes. As she thinks of the boyfriend and family she left behind, she realizes she has no one to turn to for help. (Bradbury Press, 1978)

Stranger in a Strange Land. Robert Heinlein.
The story of Valentine Michael Smith, born and educated on Mars, who arrives on our planet superhuman in abilities and ignorant of sex as we know it. He shocks the mores of Western culture by attempting to set up a strange and fascinating discipline on Earth: the first step is learning how to Grok. (G.P. Putnam's Sons, 1961)

Summer of the Monkeys. Wilson Rawls.
While exploring an Ozark river bottom with his old hound dog, Jay Berry comes upon a tree full of monkeys that have escaped from a circus. In his attempt to capture them, the boy learns not only about monkeys, but also how wishes come true. (Dell, 1977)

To Kill a Mockingbird. Harper Lee.
Small-town prejudice turns the people in a southern town against a black man accused of raping a white woman. Atticus Finch, a lawyer and the father of Scout, the storyteller, and her brother Jem, defends Tom Robinson. The children learn that standing up for what you believe in is not easy, but it is right in spite of the danger. (Harper and Row, 1960)

When the Legends Die. Hal Borland.
A young Indian finds he must leave the white world into which he was forced and return to the ways of nature and his people. The story is told by different narrators and is an experience in points of view. (Harper and Row, 1963)

Wild in the World. John Donovan.
John, a young country boy, can only watch helplessly as his brothers, sisters, mother, and father die. When his last brother dies, John buries him on their desolate mountainside. Nobody knows; no one is told. Lonely, self-sufficient, and silent, John lives alone until a stray animal—wolf or dog, he doesn't know which—decides to accept him as trustworthy. (Harper and Row, 1971)

Name _____

Date _____

Lesson One (A): Sentence Combining

FOR A START

Combine the following sentences as instructed by your teacher.

1. The board sits on a table.
2. The board is for Monopoly.
3. The board is colorful.
4. The table is in the middle of the room.

5. The board is covered with objects.
6. The objects are small.

7. Some of the objects are buildings.
8. The buildings are tiny.
9. The buildings are green.

10. Other objects are cards.
11. The cards are cardboard.
12. The cards are orange.
13. The cards are yellow.

14. There is also money.
15. The money is on the table.
16. The money is paper.
17. The money is for play.

18. The money is in two piles.
19. One pile is large.
20. One pile is small.

Here is one way to combine these sentences:

A colorful Monopoly board sits on a table in the middle of the room. The board is covered with small objects. Some of the objects are tiny green buildings. Others are orange and yellow cardboard cards. There is also paper play money on the table. The money is in two piles, one large and one small.

TRY THIS

Together with the rest of the class, combine sentences 1 to 20 in a different way. Be sure all the sentences grouped together in the list become single sentences in your combination. Do your combination on a separate piece of paper.

Lesson One (B): Sentence Combining

FOR A START

Using the space provided below, combine the following sentences into a paragraph.

1. A dish sits on a counter.
2. The counter is marble.
3. The dish is tall.
4. The dish is frosty.
5. The dish is glass.

6. The dish contains ice cream.
7. The dish contains syrup.
8. The syrup is hot.
9. The syrup is fudge.

10. On the ice cream is a glob.
11. The glob is cream
12. The cream is whipped.

13. The cream is topped.
14. The topping is nuts.
15. The topping is a cherry.
16. The cherry is red.
17. The red is bright.

TRY THIS

On a separate sheet of paper, combine the same sentences in a different way.

Name _____

Date _____

Lesson Two: Sentence Combining

FOR A START Combine these sentences on a separate piece of paper.

1. A fire engine swerves around the corner.
2. The fire engine is brilliant.
3. The brilliance is red.
4. The fire engine gleams.
5. The gleaming is in the sun.

6. A siren wails.
7. Lights flash.
8. The lights are red.
9. The lights are white.

10. The fire engine roars by.
11. The fire engine is like a beast.
12. The beast is huge.
13. The beast is important.
14. The beast is on a mission.
15. The mission is to save lives.

TRY THIS Combine these sentences on a separate piece of paper.

1. I could see a train from our automobile.
2. The train was moving fast.
3. The train was on tracks.
4. The tracks were parallel to the road.

5. Three engines pulled the train.
6. The engines were diesel.
7. The engines rumbled.
8. The rumble was loud.

9. Behind the engine was a string.
10. The string was of freight cars.
11. The string was like a snake.
12. The snake was colorful.
13. The snake was in many parts.

14. The parts were boxcars.
15. The boxcars were brown and blue.
16. The parts were flatcars.
17. The flatcars carried machines.
18. The machines were huge.
19. The parts were gondola cars.
20. The gondola cars were piled high.
21. The piling was with coal.

22. The snake's tail was a caboose.
23. The caboose was red.

24. The train passed our car.
25. The train was gone.

FOR A START

Lesson Three: Sentence Combining

Combine these sentences in the space provided below.

I remember Isabel Torres. Isabel was in my first-grade class. Isabel was my best friend. Isabel had huge eyes. The eyes were deep. The eyes were dark. The eyes always smiled. Isabel had braids. The braids were long. The braids were dark. The braids were glossy. Her clothes were usually a shirt and jeans. The shirt was plaid. The shirt was flannel. The shirt was long-sleeved. The jeans were old. The jeans were faded. The jeans were patched at the knees. The jeans were belted. The belt was crooked. Isabel could keep secrets. The secrets were about things we did. We did them alone. We did them when adults were not around.

TRY
THIS

Write a paragraph describing a friend who was special to you when you were in elementary school. Use sentences like the ones you wrote in the exercise above to show what your friend looked like and why you liked him or her.

Name _____

Date _____

Lesson Four: Sentence Combining

FOR A START Combine the following sentences into as few sentences as you can. Keep the meaning clear, avoid run-ons, and vary the beginnings of your sentences.

The waitress set down a pizza. The pizza was huge. The pizza was mouth-watering. The pizza smelled wonderful. The pizza was smothered with good things. The cheese was melted. The cheese bubbled. The cheese steamed. Sauce ran over the cheese. The sauce was made from tomatoes. The sauce was rich. The sauce was red. The sauce was flecked with bits. The bits were dark green. The bits were spices. Pepperoni was in the cheese. Sausage was in the cheese. Onions were in the cheese. The onions were green. A mug stood next to the pizza. The mug was cold. The mug was covered. The covering was droplets. The droplets were tiny. The mug was filled with ice. The mug was filled with cola. I was hungry. I dove into the pizza. Soon the pizza was gone.

TRY THIS Write a paragraph describing your favorite meal. Use the same kinds of details and sentences as you did in the exercise above.

Lesson Five: Sentence Combining

FOR A START

Combine the following sentences into as few sentences as you can. Keep the meaning clear, avoid run-ons, and vary the beginnings of your sentences.

When I was young I had a toy. The toy was my favorite. The toy was a bicycle. The bicycle was blue. The blue was glossy. The blue gleamed in the sun. I spent hours with my bike. The hours were spent riding. I rode in my neighborhood. I explored other parts of town. I sought adventures. The adventures were new. The adventures were exciting. I delivered newspapers from my bike. I pedaled up streets. I pedaled down streets. I threw papers. I threw left. I threw right. I had a feeling. The feeling was good. The feeling was of my importance. I took good care of my bike. I polished my bike. I oiled my bike. I checked the air. The air was in the tires. I loved my bike. It opened worlds. The worlds were new. The worlds were mine.

TRY THIS

Write a paragraph about a special thing you owned when you were younger. Describe it and tell why it was special, using the same kinds of details and sentences as you did in the exercise above.

Lesson Six: Sentence Combining

FOR A START Combine the following sentences into as few sentences as you can. Keep the meaning clear, avoid run-ons, and vary the beginnings of your sentences.

The boys gathered. The gathering was on a field. The field was broad. The field was green. The boys divided into two groups. The groups were teams. The teams were matched. The matching was even. The boys started to play. They played football. The teams tackled. The tackling was rough. The tackling was hard. The tackling hurt no one. The boys ran. The boys kicked. The boys passed. The boys shouted. The shouting was loud. The boys had great fun. The sun sank. The sun threw shadows. The shadows were long. The shadows were across the field. The boys stopped playing. The boys started walking. The walking was toward home. The boys were exhausted. The boys were happy.

TRY THIS Write a description of a group of your friends playing a game—either now or when you were younger. Use the same kinds of details and sentences as you did in the exercise above.

Lesson Seven: Sentence Combining

FOR A START Combine the following sentences using all the skills you have learned in earlier exercises. Keep the meaning clear, avoid run-ons, and vary the beginnings of sentences.

My father had a friend. The friend's name was Ed. Ed was a truck driver. Ed had huge hands. Ed had muscular arms. Ed had hair. The hair was thick. The hair was dark. The hair was curly. The hair was all over his body. He owned a boat. The boat was small. The boat was open. The boat was very fast. Once Ed took me for a ride. The ride was on a lake. The lake was smooth. The lake was clear. The boat roared. The boat bounced. Water sprayed. Water splashed in my face. Wind blew through my hair. We were at the point of a V. The V was across the lake. The V was formed by the boat. I liked Ed. Ed was my friend too.

TRY THIS Write a paragraph describing an adult you knew as a child. Show something you did together that explains your admiration for him or her. Use the same kinds of details and examples as you did in the exercise above.

Lesson Eight:
Major Writing Assignment

PICK A TOPIC

Your assignment is to describe a group of people. Use the kinds of sentences you have been practicing to show what happens to the group and to the people in it. Choose a topic from the ideas below.

1. shoppers and strollers at a mall

2. students in a classroom

3. people at a party

4. a family at a picnic

5. a cafeteria crowd at lunch

BEFORE YOU WRITE

The chart below is to help you gather ideas before you start writing. Pick a topic and have a specific place or group of people in mind. Next, imagine four people in the group, and think of how each would look and what each would be doing. Make notes on each person in the boxes below. Use your notes as you write your rough draft.

	Person 1	Person 2	Person 3	Person 4
A P P E A R A N C E				
A C T I V I T I E S				

Introduction to Sentence Modeling

STUDY THESE
Sentence modeling is a technique to get you to try to write different sentence structures from the ones you usually write. A variety of kinds of sentences adds to the pleasure of reading a paper. This takes practice. That's what these worksheets are for.

Example: Waiting <u>for</u> Peggy on <u>the</u> entrance steps, <u>my</u> lunch <u>in</u> <u>a</u> paper bag, <u>my</u> binder careless<u>ly</u> held, <u>I</u> watch<u>ed</u> <u>the</u> bewildered seventh graders <u>with</u> <u>a</u> <u>feeling</u> <u>of</u> greatness.
                                        —Ella Leffland, *Rumors of Peace*, p. 117.

New Version: Look<u>ing</u> <u>for</u> Jackie in <u>the</u> video store, <u>my</u> books <u>in</u> <u>a</u> green back-pack, <u>my</u> videos precarious<u>ly</u> balanced, <u>I</u> studi<u>ed</u> <u>the</u> hassled mall shoppers <u>with</u> <u>a</u> <u>feeling</u> <u>of</u> anxiety.

NOTE
Notice the Similarities:

Wait<u>ing</u> <u>for</u> Peggy Look<u>ing</u> <u>for</u> Jackie	<u>-ing</u> verb + <u>for</u> + name

on <u>the</u> entrance steps
in <u>the</u> video store
	prepositional phrase
	  (preposition + <u>the</u> + adjective +
	  noun)

<u>my</u> lunch <u>in</u> <u>a</u> paper bag <u>my</u> books <u>in</u> <u>a</u> green backpack	<u>my</u> + noun + <u>in</u> + <u>a</u> + adjective + noun
<u>my</u> binder careless<u>ly</u> held <u>my</u> videos precarious<u>ly</u> balanced	<u>my</u> + noun + adverb + past participle

<u>I</u> watch<u>ed</u> <u>the</u> bewildered seventh
  graders
<u>I</u> studi<u>ed</u> <u>the</u> hassled mall shoppers
	<u>I</u> + past-tense verb + <u>the</u> + adjective
	  + adjective + plural noun

<u>with</u> <u>a</u> <u>feeling</u> <u>of</u> greatness
<u>with</u> <u>a</u> <u>feeling</u> <u>of</u> anxiety
	prepositional phrase
	  (preposition + <u>a</u> + <u>feeling</u> + <u>of</u> +
	  abstract noun)

Sentence Modeling One

TRY THESE | Below are sentences from novels for you to model. Keep the <u>underlined</u> words and parts of words <u>exactly</u> the same. For all other words in the sentence, substitute the same kind of word or group of words. (See the introductory worksheet.) Sentence modeling requires a lot of practice. But before long, some sentences similar to these will begin to appear in your writing.

Example: <u>The</u> Negroes, <u>having</u> wait<u>ed</u> for <u>the</u> white people <u>to</u> go upstairs, <u>began</u> <u>to</u> come in.

—Harper Lee, *To Kill a Mockingbird,* p. 166.

New Version: <u>The</u> surfers, <u>having</u> paddl<u>ed</u> across <u>the</u> roaring waves <u>to</u> go out, <u>began</u> <u>to</u> ride in.

1. <u>The</u> goose-stepp<u>ing</u> troop<u>s</u> <u>were</u> reel<u>ing</u>, defeat<u>ed</u>, <u>their</u> cities bomb<u>ed</u>, <u>their</u> spirit brok<u>en</u>.

—Ella Leffland, *Rumors of Peace,* p. 127.

_____

_____

_____

2. <u>The</u> dog, <u>too</u>, <u>was</u> crouch<u>ed</u>, body slop<u>ed</u> forward, chin almost touch<u>ing</u> <u>the</u> ground.

—Robert Cormier, *I Am the Cheese,* p. 42.

_____

_____

_____

3. <u>I</u> remembered <u>the</u> <u>day</u> <u>my</u> Uncle Ted died, <u>my</u> father <u>told</u> <u>my</u> mother he <u>kept</u> hear<u>ing</u> Uncle Ted<u>'s</u> voice <u>in</u> <u>his</u> mind, hear<u>ing</u> his laugh, hear<u>ing</u> him sing, hear<u>ing</u> him tell Irish jokes.

—M.E. Kerr, *Gentlehands,* p. 126.

_____

_____

_____

22   *The Remedial Writing Teacher's Handbook*

Sentence Modeling Two

Below are sentences from novels for you to model. Keep the underlined words and parts of words exactly the same. For all other words in the sentence, substitute the same kind of word or group of words. (See the introductory worksheet.) Sentence modeling requires a lot of practice. But before long, some sentences similar to these will begin to appear in your writing.

Example: The dog is unmoving, his tail not wagging, his eyes like marbles.

—Robert Cormier, *I Am the Cheese*, p. 31.

New Version: The kitten is graceful, his body not stiffening, his limbs like feathers.

1. Thrown off balance and spinning dizzily in the air, the dog fell awkwardly to the ground, howling now, scurrying to its feet.

—Robert Cormier, *I Am the Cheese*, p. 42.

_____

_____

_____

2. I watched her. In an ordinary summer dress and no shawl she looked like anybody else, except for her walk, very fast, and with her head high.

—Ella Leffland, *Rumors of Peace*, p. 127.

_____

_____

_____

3. I wanted to tell him that I never had a time like it before, that I never knew anyone like him before, that the wine was making me float and soar and that I was so, so happy I wanted to cry.

—Fran Arrick, *Steffie Can't Come Out to Play*, p. 41.

_____

_____

_____

Sentence Modeling Three

Below are sentences from novels for you to model. Keep the underlined words and parts of words exactly the same. For all other words in the sentence, substitute the same kind of word or group of words. (See the introductory worksheet.) Sentence modeling requires a lot of practice. But before long, some sentences similar to these will begin to appear in your writing.

Example:　He open<u>ed</u> <u>the</u> door for me, <u>still</u> grinn<u>ing</u>, <u>and</u> motion<u>ed</u> me in, <u>but</u> <u>I</u> <u>was</u> <u>still</u> staring at <u>the</u> outside <u>of</u> <u>the</u> car.
　　　　　　　—Fran Arrick, *Steffie Can't Come Out to Play*, p. 16.

New Version:　She h<u>eld</u> <u>the</u> book for me, <u>still</u> wait<u>ing</u>, <u>and</u> encourag<u>ed</u> me on, <u>but</u> <u>I</u> <u>was</u> <u>still</u> shak<u>ing</u> from <u>the</u> impact <u>of</u> <u>the</u> question.

1. <u>The</u> tire bump<u>ed</u> on gravel, skeeter<u>ed</u> across <u>the</u> road, crash<u>ed</u> into <u>a</u> barrier <u>and</u> popp<u>ed</u> me <u>like</u> <u>a</u> cork onto <u>the</u> pavement.

　　　　　　　—Harper Lee, *To Kill a Mockingbird*, p. 42.

_____

_____

_____

2. They <u>had</u> left Box Canyon Boys Camp <u>at</u> eleven forty-eight <u>and</u> now, three <u>hours</u> <u>and</u> <u>a</u> bagged truck <u>and</u> some milk <u>and</u> <u>a</u> shootout later, they <u>were</u> practical<u>ly</u> there.

　　　　　　　—Glendon Swarthout, *Bless the Beasts and Children*, p. 87.

_____

_____

_____

3. I'<u>d</u> see him lean<u>ing</u> back in his chair, say<u>ing</u> his life might <u>have</u> <u>been</u> different <u>if</u> he'<u>d</u> met Carla earlier, <u>then</u> explain<u>ing</u> <u>to</u> Skye <u>that</u> birds <u>weren't</u> <u>really</u> free, <u>that</u> they <u>were</u> prisoners of their own territory.

　　　　　　　—M. E. Kerr, *Gentlehands*, p. 127.

_____

_____

_____

Sentence Modeling Four

TRY THESE Below are sentences from novels for you to model. Keep the <u>underlined</u> words and parts of words <u>exactly</u> the same. For all other words in the sentence, substitute the same kind of word or group of words. (See the introductory worksheet.) Sentence modeling requires a lot of practice. But before long, some sentences similar to these will begin to appear in your writing.

Example: <u>The</u> crowd push<u>ed</u> noisi<u>ly</u> in <u>the</u> heat <u>and</u> dust, yell<u>ing</u> at each other, clatter<u>ing</u> up <u>the</u> steel steps, into <u>the</u> train, hang<u>ing</u> out <u>the</u> open windows.

—Ella Leffland, *Rumors of Peace*, p. 127.

New Version: <u>The</u> troop hik<u>ed</u> lusti<u>ly</u> through <u>the</u> forest <u>and</u> glade sing<u>ing</u> with each other, march<u>ing</u> through <u>the</u> thick underbrush, across <u>the</u> terrain, rac<u>ing</u> with <u>the</u> frothy clouds.

1. I talk<u>ed</u> to him <u>the</u> whole time he <u>was</u> climb<u>ing</u> down, <u>just</u> <u>like</u> <u>a</u> cat <u>does</u>, backwards, <u>and</u> he made it just fine.

—Fran Arrick, *Steffie Can't Come Out to Play*, p. 45.

_____

_____

_____

2. <u>The</u> dog lift<u>s</u> his head at my approach, alert, ear<u>s</u> sharp, <u>as</u> <u>if</u> he <u>is</u> accept<u>ing</u> <u>a</u> challenge.

—Robert Cormier, *I Am the Cheese*, p. 31.

_____

_____

_____

3. Opposite them <u>was</u> <u>the</u> low, dark cube <u>of</u> <u>a</u> body shop, <u>and</u> park<u>ed</u> beside it, in shadow, <u>a</u> white Chevy pickup perhaps ten years old, <u>a</u> muddy fender-bent puddle jumper very similar to those at camp.

—Glendon Swarthout, *Bless the Beasts and Children*, p. 48.

_____

_____

_____

The Remedial Writing Teacher's Handbook

Sentence Modeling Five

TRY THESE Below are sentences from novels for you to model. Keep the underlined words and parts of words <u>exactly</u> the same. For all other words in the sentence, substitute the same kind of word or group of words. (See the introductory worksheet.) Sentence modeling requires a lot of practice. But before long, some sentences similar to these will begin to appear in your writing.

Example: <u>Already</u> he <u>had</u> begun <u>to</u> think of <u>the</u> boat <u>as</u> he thought of his <u>own</u> arms <u>and</u> legs, <u>an</u> extension <u>of</u> himself.

—Margaret Craven, *I Heard the Owl Call My Name*, p. 21.

New Version: <u>Already</u> they <u>had</u> decided <u>to</u> rely on <u>the</u> coach <u>as</u> they relied on their <u>own</u> brains <u>and</u> muscles, <u>a</u> model <u>of</u> perfection.

1. Duke came in carry<u>ing</u> <u>a</u> stepladder, glanc<u>ed</u>, look<u>ed</u> a second time, said nothing <u>and</u> set up <u>the</u> ladder.

   —Robert Heinlein, *Stranger in a Strange Land*, p. 113.

   _____

   _____

   _____

2. Nothing matter<u>ed</u> except those intervals in <u>the</u> arena when he, <u>like</u> <u>the</u> broncs them<u>selves</u>, <u>was</u> <u>a</u> fight<u>ing</u> creature wholly devo<u>ted</u> <u>to</u> punishment and self-violence.

   —Hal Borland, *When the Legends Die*, p. 205.

   _____

   _____

   _____

3. He watch<u>ed</u>, fascinated, until they <u>had</u> pass<u>ed</u> <u>and</u> for <u>a</u> moment he <u>was</u> <u>not</u> sure <u>that</u> it <u>had</u> happen<u>ed</u> at all.

   —Margaret Craven, *I Heard the Owl Call My Name*, p. 43.

   _____

   _____

   _____

Sentence Modeling Six

TRY
THESE Below are sentences from novels for you to model. Keep the <u>underlined</u> words and parts of words <u>exactly</u> the same. For all other words in the sentence, substitute the same kind of word or group of words. (See the introductory worksheet.) Sentence modeling requires a lot of practice. But before long, some sentences similar to these will begin to appear in your writing.

Example: Her father <u>is</u> editor of <u>the</u> *Monument Times* <u>and</u> always speak<u>s</u> <u>with</u> emergency in his voice, his sentences <u>like</u> headlines.

—Robert Cormier, *I Am the Cheese,* p. 6.

New Version: My sister <u>is</u> manager for <u>the</u> Carnival Computers <u>and</u> usually work<u>s</u> <u>with</u> automation in her manner, her movements <u>like</u> machinery.

1. Slowl<u>y</u>, <u>as</u> <u>the</u> needle<u>s</u> fell, <u>the</u> waters of <u>the</u> inlet grew less clear, <u>and</u> on <u>the</u> river float<u>ed</u> <u>the</u> first green leaves of <u>the</u> alders.

—Margaret Craven, *I Heard the Owl Call My Name,* p. 119.

_____

_____

_____

2. I will<u>ed</u> my<u>self</u> <u>to</u> stay awake, <u>but</u> <u>the</u> rain <u>was</u> <u>so</u> soft <u>and</u> <u>the</u> room <u>was</u> <u>so</u> warm <u>and</u> his voice <u>was</u> <u>so</u> deep <u>and</u> his knee <u>was</u> <u>so</u> snug <u>that</u> I slept.

—Harper Lee, *To Kill a Mockingbird,* p. 283.

_____

_____

_____

3. <u>Then</u> I took my hair out of <u>its</u> pony tail back <u>and</u> wrapp<u>ed</u> it up on top of my head, fasten<u>ing</u> <u>it</u> with pins, <u>and</u> leav<u>ing</u> little wisps of hair hang<u>ing</u> down in back <u>and</u> on <u>the</u> sides.

—Fran Arrick, *Steffie Can't Come Out to Play,* p. 35.

_____

_____

_____

Sentence Modeling Seven

TRY THESE

Below are sentences from novels for you to model. Keep the underlined words and parts of words exactly the same. For all other words in the sentence, substitute the same kind of word or group of words. (See the introductory worksheet.) Sentence modeling requires a lot of practice. But before long, some sentences similar to these will begin to appear in your writing.

Example: Alone now, with a brief moment of freedom from the constant daytime urging, the old dog made the most of it.
—Sheila Burnford, *The Incredible Journey*, p. 56.

New Version: Alone now, in a rare spell of seclusion free from the steady childish chattering, the young mother enjoyed the serenity of it.

1. Her face was plump and smooth, with sharp brown eyes, her thick brown hair swept carelessly into a bun, her heavy figure clad in a brown cotton skirt and black turtleneck sweater.

—Ella Leffland, *Rumors of Peace*, p. 176.

_____

_____

_____

2. Seconds later, the old dog caught the scent too, and started to his feet, snuffing and questioning with his nose.

—Sheila Burnford, *The Incredible Journey*, p. 43.

_____

_____

_____

3. When they got to his mother's grave, even though they didn't walk anymore, the sound of the leaves crackling underfoot remained in Jonny's mind.

—John Donovan, *Wild in the World*, p. 61.

_____

_____

_____

Sentence Modeling Eight

Below are sentences from novels for you to model. Keep the underlined words and parts of words exactly the same. For all other words in the sentence, substitute the same kind of word or group of words. (See the introductory worksheet.) Sentence modeling requires a lot of practice. But before long, some sentences similar to these will begin to appear in your writing.

Example: Mumbl<u>ing</u> <u>something</u> about <u>a</u> yell<u>ing</u> boy <u>and</u> <u>a</u> bawling hound, Granpa <u>finally</u> <u>got</u> <u>the</u> mares settl<u>ed</u> down.
                        —Wilson Rawls, *Summer of the Monkeys*, p. 160.

New Version: Throw<u>ing</u> <u>something</u> between <u>a</u> laugh<u>ing</u> child <u>and</u> <u>a</u> bored parent, Sam <u>finally</u> <u>got</u> <u>the</u> family relax<u>ed</u> together.

1. <u>The</u> <u>only</u> <u>thing</u> she <u>could</u> hear now, <u>except</u> <u>for</u> Robbie's muffled laughter, <u>was</u> <u>the</u> rustle <u>of</u> leaves blow<u>ing</u> along <u>the</u> sidewalk <u>that</u> led to <u>the</u> Turners' front porch forty feet in front of them.

                        —Robin F. Brancato, *Something Left to Lose*, p. 3.

_____

_____

_____

2. <u>Then</u> dropp<u>ing</u> <u>the</u> tin can he <u>was</u> hold<u>ing</u> in his paw, he reach<u>ed</u> over <u>and</u> took <u>the</u> apple from my hand.

                        —Wilson Rawls, *Summer of the Monkeys*, p. 132.

_____

_____

3. He <u>was</u> swept <u>with</u> <u>a</u> sadness, <u>a</u> sadness deep <u>and</u> penetrating, leav<u>ing</u> him desolate <u>like</u> someone wash<u>ed</u> up on a beach, <u>a</u> lone survivor in <u>a</u> world full <u>of</u> strangers.

                        —Robert Cormier, *The Chocolate War*, p. 124.

_____

_____

_____

Sentence Modeling Nine

Below are sentences from novels for you to model. Keep the <u>underlined</u> words and parts of words <u>exactly</u> the same. For all other words in the sentence, substitute the same kind of word or group of words. (See the introductory worksheet.) Sentence modeling requires a lot of practice. But before long, some sentences similar to these will begin to appear in your writing.

Example: Fadin<u>g</u> back, he pick<u>ed</u> (up) <u>a</u> decent block <u>and</u> cock<u>ed</u> his arm, searchi<u>ng</u> for <u>a</u> receiver—<u>maybe the</u> tall kid <u>they call The Goober</u>.

        —Robert Cormier, *The Chocolate War*, p. 4.

New Version: Swervi<u>ng</u> around, he execut<u>ed</u> <u>a</u> fantastic turn <u>and</u> tens<u>ed</u> his body, watchi<u>ng</u> for <u>an</u> obstacle—<u>maybe the</u> deep hole <u>they call The</u> Sink.

4. Caroni watch<u>ed</u> <u>the</u> chalk <u>in</u> Brother Leon's hands, <u>the way the</u> teacher press<u>ed</u> <u>it</u>, roll<u>ed</u> <u>it</u>, his fingers <u>like the</u> legs <u>of</u> pale spiders <u>with</u> <u>a</u> victim in their clutch.

        —Robert Cormier, *The Chocolate War*, p. 105.

_____

_____

_____

5. Duke came in carryi<u>ng</u> <u>a</u> step ladder, glanc<u>ed</u>, look<u>ed</u> <u>a</u> second time, said nothing <u>and</u> set (up) <u>the</u> ladder.

        —Robert Heinlein, *Stranger in a Strange Land*, p. 113.

_____

_____

_____

6. Tom <u>tried to</u> tell him about <u>the</u> big circuit, <u>where</u> he <u>had</u> been, <u>what</u> he <u>had</u> done, <u>and</u> especially about Albuquerque, <u>which</u> he <u>was</u> sure Meo <u>would</u> understand.

        —Hal Borland, *When the Legends Die,* p. 187.

_____

_____

_____

Sentence Modeling Ten

Below are sentences from novels for you to model. Keep the underlined words and parts of words exactly the same. For all other words in the sentence, substitute the same kind of word or group of words. (See the introductory worksheet.) Sentence modeling requires a lot of practice. But before long, some sentences similar to these will begin to appear in your writing.

Example: Above their heads, attrac<u>ted</u> <u>by</u> <u>the</u> firelight, <u>a</u> storm <u>of</u> white moths flew about <u>like</u> summer snow.
—Robert Newton Peck, *Fawn*, p. 84.

New Version: Below his feet, aler<u>ted</u> <u>by</u> <u>the</u> engine, <u>a</u> group <u>of</u> forest rangers ra<u>ced</u> around <u>like</u> frenzied fireflies.

1. He let it ring awhile, <u>while</u> his thoughts ra<u>ced</u> <u>and</u> cross<u>ed</u> each other, <u>until</u> they became <u>a</u> whirl <u>and</u> <u>a</u> searching.
—Jay Bennett, *Say Hello to the Hit Man*, p. 94.

_____

_____

_____

2. <u>The</u> other bus boys, <u>who</u> <u>had</u> <u>been</u> hunch<u>ed</u> over their plates <u>like</u> quarterbacks gett<u>ing</u> <u>the</u> captain's signals, now straightened.
—Betty Smith, *Joy in the Morning*, p. 35.

_____

_____

_____

3. His left arm <u>was</u> somewhat shorter than his right; <u>when</u> he stood <u>or</u> walk<u>ed</u>, <u>the</u> back <u>of</u> his hand <u>was</u> at right angles to his body, his thumb parallel to his thigh.
—Harper Lee, *To Kill a Mockingbird*, p. 7.

_____

_____

_____

Chapter 3

The Paragraph

Coordinate, Subordinate, and Mixed Sequences

In this chapter, your students will learn to structure various types of paragraphs while at the same time they practice composing different types of sentence structures. The numbering system that follows is based on Chris Honore's adaptation of Francis Christiansen's explanations in *Notes Toward a New Rhetoric* (Harper and Row, 1978). The numbering system has been very successful with the students we have worked with in remedial composition; we offer it as one approach to the teaching of the paragraph and, later, the essay.

The goal in the instruction of writing the paragraph is to teach students how to think on paper, how to defend their ideas on paper, and how to defend their ideas later in life.

The topic sentence of the paragraph is designated the #2 sentence. This sentence is, of course, the thesis, hypothesis, or opinion to be explained by the following sentences. The #2 sentence is **generalized**; the sentences that follow will be more **specific**.

Coordinate. In the **coordinate sequence**, each sentence that follows the #2 is more specific than the #2 sentence. Each of these sentences is called a #3 sentence, **coordinate** to each other in importance, **subordinate** to the #2 sentence.

In the following coordinate sequence paragraph, the sentences have been numbered in order to aid in explanation, which is the main reason for the use of the numbers. It is, of course, the teacher's decision to use or not to use the numbering technique. We have found that with the writers who have very serious problems the numbering is a definite help. Another suggestion is to present the coordinate sequence as a parallel to the view through the **wide-angle lens** of a camera, in which no one element is more in focus than any other; similarly, the #3 sentences are coordinates of each other.

> #2 There are three ingredients, police say, that combine to make a home highly burglar resistant. #3 Neighbors who are curious about what's going on outside their front lawn comprise the first. #3 Locks that meet certain specifications are the second deterrent. #3 And valuables that are engraved with your driver's license number are the third.
>
> From Sheila Stavish, "Shoestring Security," *Plus,* Spring 1981, p. 2.

Subordinate. In the **subordinate sequence**, each sentence that follows the #2 is more specific than the #2 sentence *and more specific than the preceding sentence.* Since each sentence further explains the one before it, the numbering sequence progresses like so: #2, #3, #4, #5, #6, etc. As in the coordinate sequence, each sentence following the #2 is **subordinate** to the #2; in addition, each sentence is subordinate to the one immediately preceding it.

In the following subordinate sequence paragraph, the sentences have been numbered in order to aid in explanation. Again, it is your decision whether to use the numbers or the terminology alone. And again, we recommend the combination of verbal and numerical explanation. A camera analogy for the subordinate sequence is also helpful. Tell the writers to imagine that they are looking through a **zoom lens**, b]eginning with a wide or broad view and focusing on more and more detail as they zoom in. Thus, the subordinate sequence of 2–3–4–5–6–7–etc., moves from a generalized view to a highly specific one.

> #2 As I watched, the young boy played in the sandbox. #3 His whole torso concentrated on the castle he was building. #4 Creating and protecting the castle walls, his tanned arms deftly fenced in the entire structure. #5 His small but purposeful left hand scooped wet sand from a bucket on his side, dribbling it to design turrets as the right hand protectively patted all in place.

Mixed Sequence. Most paragraphs are neither coordinate nor subordinate sequences, but **mixed sequence** paragraphs, in order to provide the depth of explanation needed to satisfy the reader. The mixed sequence paragraph has no definite order; it varies according to the ideas to be expressed. What is constant is the #2 sentence, #3 sentences that are **subordinate** to the #2 and **coordinate** to each other, and more specific sentences subordinate to the #3 sentences as needed.

Following is a sample paragraph in mixed sequence:

> #2 Berkeley, California, is a special place to live, offering a variety of advantages to almost anyone. #3 For those culturally inclined, the University of California provides a wide range of events. #4 Music, drama, films, and lectures are offered weekly by the Committee on Arts and Lectures. #5 Within each of these areas, a range is provided, as last week's country-music festival and this week's classical symphony exhibit. #3 Those interested in sports will find excellent facilities for themselves and their friends. #4 In addition to actually playing games such as tennis, handball, racquetball, and golf, there are numerous opportunities for sports enthusiasts to be spectators. #3 Berkeley's mild climate is nearly ideal. #4 It never gets very cold, and the summers are never too hot. #5 Each day from June through September the fog rolls in off San Francisco Bay to keep the temperature down. #3 But the best thing about Berkeley is the people. #4 People from all over the world have gathered there because of the university, and many have stayed. #5 The result is a population of many backgrounds and nationalities.

The following worksheet lessons will give your students practice in identifying and organizing sequences. We recommend that you prepare your students carefully and go over the Introductory Worksheet (page 34) in detail before assigning any of the lessons.

Answer Key

Lesson One

A. 2, 3, 3, 3

B. 2, 3, 4

Lesson Two

A. Mixed
2, 3, 3, 4, 5

B. Coordinate
2, 3, 3, 3

C. Subordinate
2, 3, 4, 5, 6

Lesson Three

A. Coordinate
2, 3, 3, 3, 3

B. Subordinate
Jean Baptiste Lamarck . . .
Lamarckism holds that . . .
Lamarck thought that . . .
He thought that . . .

C. Mixed

Sequences

FOR A START

Write the meanings of the following terms:

A. #2 sentence _____

_____

B. coordinate _____

_____

C. subordinate _____

_____

D. general _____

_____

E. specific _____

_____

F. #3 sentence _____

_____

G. #4, #5, #6, etc., sentences _____

_____

STUDY THESE

Sample Paragraphs

• **Coordinate Sequence**

#2 There are three ingredients, police say, that combine to make a home highly burglar resistant. #3 Neighbors who are curious about what's going on outside their front lawn comprise the first. #3 Locks that meet certain specifications are the second deterrent. #3 And valuables that are engraved with your driver's license number are the third.

—Sheila Stavish, "Shoestring Security," *Plus*, Spring 1981, p. 2.

• **Subordinate Sequence**

#2 As I watched, the young boy played in the sandbox. #3 His whole torso concentrated on the castle he was building. #4 Creating and protecting the castle walls, his tanned arms deftly fenced in the entire structure. #5 His small but purposeful left hand scooped wet sand from a bucket on his side, dribbling it to design turrets as the right hand protectively patted all in place.

Name _____

Date _____

Lesson One

FOR A START

Number the sentences below according to the explanation of coordinate and subordinate sequences. See the Introductory Sheet, "Sequences," for help.

A. _____ My three brothers are as different as they could possibly be. _____ John is a doctor who lives in Florida and water-skis. _____ Tim enjoys his construction job in the Midwest and lifts weights in his spare time. _____ And Mike spends his time either making leather moccasins or belts or hiking in the High Sierras.

B. _____ The thing that most concerns scientists who view marijuana as dangerous is that THC and the compounds produced from it do not dissolve in water, and so are not flushed out of the body as easily as alcohol or caffeine. _____ Instead, the compounds mix with internal fat deposits, and may linger in their plump fat pockets for as long as two weeks. _____ These fat deposits are found in some chemically sensitive areas—the brain, the hormone-producing adrenal glands, the ovaries or testes, and the placenta of a pregnant woman.

—Natalie Angier, "Marijuana: Bad News and Good,"
Discover, August 1981, p. 16.

Coordinate Sequence

TRY THIS

Now create a paragraph according to the coordinate sequence approach. Be sure each #3 supports the #2 and is parallel to the other #3's—none more specific than the others. (Think of how the wide-angle lens of a camera keeps everything equally in focus.)

#2 _____

_____

#3 _____

_____

#3 _____

_____

#3 _____

_____

#3 _____

_____

(continued)

Lesson One *(continued)*

Subordinate Sequence

> **TRY THIS**

Now create your own paragraph according to the subordinate sequence approach. Make sure that each sentence following the #2 is more specific than the one before it and that each one is specifically about the one before it. (Think of how the zoom lens of a camera moves in closer and closer to the subject.)

#2 _____

_____

#3 _____

_____

#4 _____

_____

#5 _____

_____

#6 _____

_____

> **NOW THIS**

Exchange papers with another student in the class. Evaluate each other's papers. Evaluator's comments (be specific to help the writer):

COORDINATE SEQUENCE _____

_____

_____

_____

SUBORDINATE SEQUENCE _____

_____

_____

_____

The Remedial Writing Teacher's Handbook

Lesson Two

TRY THESE

Identify the types of sequences for each paragraph (coordinate, subordinate, or mixed). Then number the sentences below according to their sequence.

A. _____ **Sequence**

_____ Julia Morgan, the architect who designed Hearst Castle near San Simeon, California, is best remembered for this work so totally different from her other structures. _____ Her architectural credo was "Buildings should be unobtrusive elements on a landscape"; yet Hearst Castle is far from unobtrusive. _____ She also believed that the architect's responsibility is to serve the client. _____ William Randolph Hearst wanted "a small cluster of buildings where my friends can come and enjoy my collection." _____ The modest cluster grew steadily into what came to be called a castle, a major tourist attraction in California.

> —"Julia Morgan—The Architect Behind the Castle," PG and E Progress, June 1981, p. 8.

B. _____ **Sequence**

_____ Few modern artists have succeeded at being truly modern and pleasing the general public as well as Red Grooms, a 43-year-old teenager from Nashville. _____ His model of his adopted city, "Ruckus Manhattan," installed in the Marlborough Gallery, reflects his view of the way things are, crazy, funny. _____ His paintings, "Danny's Hero Sandwich" and "Looking Along Broadway Towards Grace Church," reveal both his humor and his relaxed, humane attitude toward life. _____ In all his work, Grooms is sharply satirical but never mean, saying everybody and everything is funny looking, so nobody need be ashamed of it.

> —"Painting the Town Red," *Newsweek*, April 20, 1981, p. 86.

C. _____ **Sequence**

_____ Dr. D. Carlton Gajdusek, an American epidemiologist, investigated in 1957 the reason a small tribe in New Guinea, the Fore, was threatened with extinction. _____ For unknown reasons, most of its women were being attacked by a nerve disease that began in giggles and ended in death. _____ Dr. Gajdusek treated the patients with every medicine he could find, and he checked the water, the soil, even the cooking ashes. _____ Finally he found that when someone died, the Fore buried the corpse, then, as a way of preserving his spirit, his relatives dug him up and ate selected portions. _____ Nothing might happen for years, but eventually the women, who were the main participants in this ritual, started the fatal giggles.

> —Gerald Clarke, "The Most Dangerous Game," *Time*, June 16, 1980, p. 51.

Lesson Three

FOR A START

Number the sentences in the following paragraph. Then decide which type of sequence the sentences are written in.

A. _____ **Sequence**

_____ In 1979 Dennis Matteson of Manhattan, Kansas, built an electronically powered motorcycle, the slowest, quietest Harley-Davidson 250 Sprint around. _____ Gone is the Harley's four stroke gasoline engine, and in its place lives a 125 pound pack of lead acid batteries and a 200 amp aircraft starter producing about five horsepower. _____ This modified bike weighs about fifty pounds over the original machine. _____ The bike reaches a top speed of 35 m.p.h. _____ Matteson's Harley must, of course, be recharged every night.

—"The Wallsocket Flyer," *Cycle*, July 1980, p. 18.

TRY THIS

Rearrange the following sentences to form a well-composed paragraph. Then decide which type of sequence the sentences are written in.

> Lamarckism holds that traits acquired during a creature's lifetime can be passed on to its offspring.
>
> He thought that environmental demands, like the need to reach for higher foliage, directed hereditary change.
>
> Lamarck thought that a giraffe, for example, could increase the length of its neck by stretching it to reach high leaves, and pass on that acquired characteristic—the longer neck—to its offspring.
>
> Jean Baptiste Lamarck, an eighteenth century botanist, proposed a theory of evolution more than fifty years before Darwin.

B. _____ **Sequence**

_____

_____

_____

_____

_____

_____

_____

—James Gorman, "Born Again Lamarckism," *Discover*, August 1981, p. 21.

(continued)

Lesson Three *(continued)*

Now This > Select one of the statements below as your #2 sentence.

The best movie I have seen lately is _____ .

My favorite television program is _____ .

My most interesting neighbor is _____ .

Then think of two #3 sentences and one #4 sentence to complete the paragraph. Make them good sentences, not short, choppy ones. Study the two sequences below and decide which you will follow. Circle your choice.

#2   #2

　　#3   #3

　　　#4   or   #3

　　#3   #4

Write your paragraph here. Identify the type of sequence.

C. _____ **Sequence**

_____

_____

_____

_____

_____

_____

_____

_____

Kinds of Paragraphs

The following lessons, which involve writing various different kinds of paragraphs, are designed to follow the discussion and understanding of coordinate, subordinate, and mixed sequence paragraphs. The numbering and terminology may be used together, or you may elect to use only the terminology. We recommend the combined approach as especially useful with remedial writers.

> *Note:* There are no reproducible worksheets provided for these lessons. That is because you and your students will be generating and building on your own materials to a large extent here. We do, however, provide some suggestions which you can transfer to a chalkboard or handout as needed.

Developing a Paragraph

Explain to your students that they now have a basic understanding of the ways in which a paragraph can be constructed—by coordination, by subordination, and by mixing the two. Now it is time to learn how to apply this knowledge in writing different kinds of paragraphs. The next seventeen lessons will focus on types of paragraphs with teacher explanation, examples, exercises, and tests.

Lesson One (Using Examples). In the example type of paragraph, a topic sentence, the #2, makes a statement, and the remaining sentences of the paragraph give **examples** to support the #2. The examples are the #3 sentences and are coordinate to each other, equally important in the paragraph. (After the students have created the example paragraph in a 2–3–3–3–3 format, you will have them write the same paragraph as a mixed sequence in which the examples, #3's, are more fully explained by the #4's and #5's. Withhold this future strategy until after the simple example paragraphs have been developed.)

On the board, write a #2 sentence the whole class can help in developing. Some suggestions:

A. There are many fine restaurants in _____ County [or in the area in which you teach, or in a certain city].

B. _____ High School offers several courses [or activities] for students interested in _____ .

C. Several cars that have been introduced during the last twenty-five years have made a difference in _____ .

D. Although many people think breakfast is a boring meal, it can be an interesting one if you vary the menu.

E. In this community, the teenagers have several favorite spots.

F. In this town, there are quite a few styles of architecture to be seen.

Tell the students to help you write the example paragraph by brainstorming ideas for you to jot on a section of the chalkboard. Give no guidelines yet; just jot down students' ideas. Sentence form or lack of it is not important at this stage. After the ideas are on the board in note form, give the following guidelines for the actual formation of the #3 example sentences.

A. Include in the sentences the name of the restaurant, the location (city, county, or area), and the atmosphere or decor.

B. Mention in each sentence either the name of the course or organization, the instructor or sponsor, and a phrase about the content of the course or purpose of the organization.

C. Include the names of the cars, the makes of the cars, the years they were introduced (if possible), and what their influence has been.

D. Describe a completely different kind of breakfast in each sentence.

E. Mention the location of each spot, the name if it has one, the way in which teenagers congregate (car, motorcycle, in-line skates, skateboards, on foot, etc.), and the activity they pursue or interest they share in that spot.

F. Name the building, the location, and the type of architecture, and add a phrase of description (or just write the phrase of description) in each sentence.

> *Note:* Some students will be able to compose such sentences mentally, while others will have to write on paper before offering them orally. Try to include as many students as possible in composing the paragraph orally.

As the students volunteer to compose the four to six #3 sentences you need to complete the paragraph on the board, you can:

1. Show them, as you write on the board, how to vary the sentence patterns while still carefully including all the information. Explain that this technique helps to prevent the paragraph from becoming boring.

2. Show them how to select **active** verbs whenever possible, instead of **passive** verbs, to liven up their writing.

3. Above all, encourage student participation and rave about the paragraph of examples that they helped you construct. This may sound very elementary, but remedial writing students will have rarely expended this much effort, thought, or energy on the writing of a single paragraph!

4. Require each student to copy the paragraph exactly as it is into his or her notes on paragraphs in a special section entitled "Sample Paragraphs."

Lesson Two (Using Examples). Have the class generate the #2 sentences for five example paragraphs. Each student must select one #2 sentence and compose the rest of the paragraph individually. You designate the number of sentences. This may be a homework assignment following Lesson One.

When the students have completed their paragraphs, have them exchange papers for evaluation. On the bottom third of the paper being evaluated, they are to write responses to the following (put on board or on handouts):

1. Evaluator's name.

2. Do the #3 sentences following the #2 sentence give examples to further explain the #2? If not all, be precise in your answer.

3. Are the #3 sentences different enough to make the paragraph interesting?

4. If your answer to question 3 is no, what is your advice to the writer in forming the #3 sentences?

   A. Try rearranging the information within the sentences for some variety.

   B. Instead of **being** verbs, try using **action** verbs like **is, was, were, seem.**

   C. Try using other vocabulary words you know.

   D. Try being more specific—not so general—in naming things.

Have students return papers to owners after you have glanced at the paragraphs to make sure that everyone understood what to do.

Lesson Three (Using Examples). Return student paragraphs of examples, explaining that these are paragraphs in coordinate sequence (2–3–3–3– etc.). Tell them that to add more depth to the writing, to explain more fully, a mixed sequence would be the method to try.

Have students designate with a mark at the beginning of each #3 sentence the ones they could explain more completely in order to better illustrate the #2 idea. Since students will be revising from a coordinate to a mixed sequence, they may wish to pull some of the details of their #3 sentences and incorporate those details into #4 or #5 sentences. Not every #3 sentence must be developed more fully. Students are then to work in class on the creation of the mixed sequence version of the previous lesson's coordinate sequence paragraph of examples. Both the coordinate and the mixed sequence version will be considered in evaluation and collected the next day.

Again, students will exchange papers for evaluation, commenting according to your questions from Lesson Two on the board or handout. Evaluation will occur on the following day.

Lesson Four (Using Examples). Each student is to exchange both coordinate and mixed sequence paragraphs of examples with another student. Students are to evaluate papers according to the following instructions. (If there is a second draft of the coordinate paragraph, evaluators should consider the second draft instead of the first.) Put on the board or on a handout:

1. Evaluator's name.

2. Did the writer select more than one sentence from the coordinate sequence to explain more fully? [Vary this question according to your demands about quantity.]

3. Did each #4 sentence directly refer to the #3 before it? If no, be precise in your answer; tell where the problem is.

4. What advice do you have about sentence structures? [See A through D in evaluation question 4, Lesson Two.]

Return papers to the original writers before collecting them to be recorded. Collect all versions so you can see the change from the coordinate to the mixed sequence. If possible, check the papers in class as the students are writing, eliminating the need for collecting papers. Collect the papers only after the writers have had time to read the evaluators' responses and to attempt a second draft if they received comments of no to evaluation question 3 and advice on evaluation question 4.

Lesson Five (Using Reasons). In this type of paragraph, a statement is made in the topic sentence—the #2—and the #3 sentences give **reasons** to support the idea. These #3 sentences are coordinate to each other, equally important within the paragraph. After your students have created the "reason" paragraphs in a 2–3–3–3–3– etc. format, they will then write the paragraphs in a mixed sequence format.

Follow the same procedure as you did for the example paragraphs, beginning with the placement of a strong #2 statement on the board. Then ask students to brainstorm ideas and help you to complete the paragraph.

Here are some ideas for the #2 sentences of paragraphs to be developed using reasons:

A. English should/should not be required during all four years of high school.

B. The draft is/is not the right way to build up the armed forces in this country.

C. Women should/should not hold combat positions in the military.

D. Teenagers who work and live at home should/should not contribute financially to their households.

E. Religious beliefs and philosophy should/should not change with the times.

F. Teenage pregnancy and parenthood is/is not becoming more acceptable.

G. High schools should/should not have extra-curricular programs.

H. *Christian Conservative* magazine should/should not be in the high school library.

Create the paragraph on the board as the students supply you with (1) the reasons in note form, and (2) the fully developed sentences. You can eliminate the note form and proceed directly to the formation of the #3 sentences of reasons if the class is ready.

Make sure that the students do not explain too much in their #3 sentences, allowing them only a short **because** clause. The wiser ones will see that you are saving the more specific explanations for the #4's and #5's to come in the second part of this assignment.

Have the students copy the paragraph into their notes as a sample of paragraph development using reasons.

Lesson Six (Using Reasons). See Lesson Two. Use the composition phase as homework. Make necessary changes in evaluation question 2 for reasons in place of examples.

Lesson Seven (Using Reasons). See Lesson Three. This will follow during class the quick Lesson Six evaluation of homework paragraphs.

Lesson Eight (Using Reasons). See Lesson Four. This should take about ten minutes by this stage.

Lesson Nine (Using Comparison/Contrast). In this type of paragraph, the statement made in the #2 sentence compares or contrasts two or more things. To **compare** is to show how two things are alike; to **contrast** is to show how they are different. The rest of the sentences support the statement made in the #2 sentence. There are several ways to approach a paragraph that compares or contrasts. It is usually better to attempt to do one or the other in one paragraph, rather than to try to do both.

Consider the #2 statement below:

> The trimester system is better than the semester system in education.

The sentences that follow the #2 will show how the two systems are different, also pointing out that one is better than the other.

Observe the approach in the following paragraph:

> #2 The trimester system is better than the semester system in education. #3A The trimester term of classes is necessarily shorter, since there are three in one school year. #3B The semester system has two longer terms. #4 A student is less likely to be bored in the shorter, faster-paced trimester approach. #3A The school facility is used practically year-round in the trimester system, since a summer trimester is attended by many students. #3B Most schools on a semester system are vacant after the second semester for two and a half months of summer vacation. #4 Because of the year-round usage of the plant, the trimester system is both more energy saving and more economical than the semester approach. #3A The trimester system allows a student the opportunity to attend school year-round. #3B The semester system offers two sessions of classes only. #4 For students who wish to finish school earlier, the trimester system allows full-year opportunities, whereas the semester system necessitates a long summer vacation.

That same paragraph could be written with the #3A's and #3B's as the #4's, and the #4's as the #3's.

The third approach requires some board work, a lot of explaining, and actual writing practice. Show the students how to combine elements in the two versions above into one sentence. Certain transitional words will be introduced at this point.

Example:

> #3A The trimester system allows a student the opportunity to attend school year-round.
> #3B The semester system offers two sessions of classes only.
> #4 For students who wish to finish school earlier, the trimester system allows full-year opportunities, whereas the semester system necessitates a long summer vacation.

Whereas the semester system offers only two class sessions, the trimester plan allows a student to attend three sessions in one year. **Therefore**, a student who wants to finish earlier would benefit front the trimester plan.

Or:

Whereas the semester system offers only two class sessions, the trimester plan allows a student to attend three sessions in one year, **thereby** becoming the better choice for the student who wants to finish school earlier.

The technique of combining elements into a longer, more complex sentence is one that some of the remedial writing students will be ready to try. You will have to determine whether to present the combined sentences approach to the whole class or only to part of the class. Again, both the board and a handout would work well to accomplish this part of the lesson.

Even without combining, the choice of the first two ways to write the paragraph (2–3A–3B–4 or 2–3–4A–4B) offers some variety and requires a plan on the student's part both before and while writing.

Here are some ideas for the #2 sentences for paragraphs of comparison or contrast:

A. The Chevy is a better car than the Ford [or vice versa].

B. Because of real seasonal changes, living in _____ [a northern city] is very different from living in _____ [San Francisco/Miami/another temperate city].

C. The teenagers in _____ are very much like the teenagers in _____ [two cities, countries, or schools; use unlike if you wish].

D. Mothers and fathers play quite different roles in most families.

E. Having two parents working instead of only one results in a very different household routine [or family situation].

F. Living in a one-parent family is very different from living in a two-parent family.

Lesson Ten (Using Comparison/Contrast). This lesson should be assigned as homework **only if it is begun in class.** Because it is more complicated than the previous types of paragraphs, you should be sure each student knows not only what is going to be written about but which approach will be taken.

Have each student select one of the given #2 sentences for the paragraph of comparison or contrast. Be sure the paper is titled either Comparison Paragraph or Contrast Paragraph, so you will know whether or not the student understands the terminology, the meaning of comparison and contrast. Have the students number each sentence with a small numeral, either after finishing (the better writers, for a self-check) or while writing (the struggling writers, for a plan to follow).

Lesson Eleven (Using Comparison/Contrast). Give these directions to your class: Exchange papers of comparison or contrast paragraphs. Today's exchange of paragraphs is a quiz. Do not write anything on the other person's paper except your own name in the bottom right corner plus the word **evaluator**. On a separate paper put your name in the top right corner [or where you usually have your students head their papers]. Before you write anything else, read the entire paragraph through once. Now you are ready to evaluate. Read the questions on the board. Answer each and follow each direction on your paper for a quiz grade.

1. Is the paragraph the type of paragraph that the writer has labeled it as (either comparison or contrast)?

2. Is the paragraph numbered appropriately for the writer's pattern of sentences? [Or, if you are not using numbers: Is the paragraph orderly in its pattern of sentences?]

3. If yes to question 2, explain in your words how the sentences are organized. Be very clear in your explanation.

4. If no to question 2, rewrite the paragraph, arranging the sentences in an orderly, consistent pattern. Make any necessary changes in wording and spelling. [If you are using numbers: Number the sentences for the original writer to see.]

This is the time in the lesson when you decide whether to move rapidly around the room, scanning original paragraphs and checking evaluators' responses, or whether to collect. If a good teaching assistant is available, you can both begin the checking during class. If a good teaching assistant is available to work for you during the school day, provide him or her with the evaluation questions above and a copy of your sample numbered paragraph on trimester/semester, along with alternate approaches. A trained student assistant can really be helpful in handling the writings of this class.

Lesson Twelve (Using Comparison/Contrast). One more attempt at comparison or contrast is important. Have the students create their own #2 sentences, selecting the type of paragraph they

didn't write for the last lesson. That is, if they wrote a comparison paragraph, have them try a contrast paragraph, or vice versa.

If this takes half of the period, select the better paragraphs for students to write on the board or read aloud. Spend what time is available on analyzing the paragraphs orally. Collect all papers for credit.

Lesson Thirteen (Using Cause/Effect). Like the comparison or contrast paragraph, the cause and effect paragraph requires important prewriting decisions because it may be organized in two different ways. In the first method, a situation or "cause" is set forth in the #2 sentence. Several #3 sentences of effects are then added, each including subordinate sentences (#4, #5, etc.) to explain them.

Consider the following example:

> #2 The recent layoffs of 350 workers at the Adams Shoe Factory have had effects on many people other than those who lost their jobs. #3 Sam's Sandwich Shop, across the street from the Adams factory, has seen its business drop by 50 percent. #4 Sam's is selling 200 fewer sandwiches at each lunchtime. #5 At an average price of $2.00 per sandwich, that's a loss of $400 in sales per day. #3 Another business affected by the layoff is Kiddie Kare, a popular day-care center. #4 Laid-off parents who used to send their offspring to Kiddie Kare are now looking after the children at home. #5 "How can I afford day care when I'm out of a job?" asks former Adams worker Brenda Starr. #4 The drop in attendance at Kiddie Kare in turn has resulted in several day-care workers joining the ranks of the laid-off.

The #2 sentence states the cause. The #3 sentences give the effects. The #4 and #5 sentences more explicitly explain the #3 and #4 sentences, respectively.

The paragraph could be reversed so that the effects are given first. The #2 statement is saved for the end, with a bit more punch added.

Consider this cause and effect paragraph in which there are several causes and one main effect:

#3 Nearly 5000 cases of child abuse were reported in Center County in 1995, and it has been estimated that for every beaten child who receives help, another twelve do not. #3 But Sister Susan Ann Weltz of the Sisters of Saint Joseph decided to work on an option for parents who feel they may be pressured into beating their children. #4 After abandoning her search for a house in Oakland, she found a house in Berkeley, but discovered it could not meet fire and safety regulations. #4 She then decided to try the Concord area, where city planners and fire inspectors helped her find a suitable house. #5 The owner not only sold her the property; he also helped her obtain use permits and necessary zoning changes. #5 The project met no opposition from government agencies, and the County Board of Supervisors authorized a $20,000 grant from revenue sharing funds for child services. #5 Donations from charities and other groups made up the rest of the $25,000 down payment. #2 Because of all this, the Bay Area Crisis Nursery at Mendocino Drive and Clayton Road in Concord will provide a temporary home for infants and preschoolers whose parents wish to place them there temporarily while the parents try to work out their problems.

The #3 sentences give the causes. The #4 and #5 sentences explain the causes and the steps they involved. The #2 sentence gives the effect at the end.

The paragraph could be switched around so that the #2, the effect, comes first, with the #3's, #4's, and #5's following as the causes and their explanations. Here are some topic ideas for the paragraphs of cause and effect:

A. A state cutback in educational spending has caused some changes in this school. (one cause, several effects)

B. The mini boom in babies born to baby boomers is now showing its effect(s). (one cause, one or more effects)

C. Several factors led to the Civil War between the North and the South. (one effect, several causes)

D. Most young married couples cannot afford to buy a house today in the United States. (one effect, several causes)

Lesson Fourteen. (Using Cause/Effect). This lesson should be assigned as homework **only if it is begun in class**. Cause and effect, like comparison or

contrast, is more complicated for the remedial writer than the earlier types of paragraphs.

Have each student select one of the given #2 sentences for a cause-and-effect paragraph. Be sure the students understand their respective plans of attack: Does the paragraph begin with several causes and lead to the effect? Or does it lead to several effects? Or does it begin with one cause and lead to several effects? Or does it begin with the single effect and then present the causes? Or does it possibly take an approach not mentioned? It will be helpful if the writer understands his or her approach and can explain it to you either orally or in writing. Again, use the numbers if they are helpful. If the numbers get in the way, disregard them for this session.

Lesson Fifteen (Using Cause/Effect). See Lesson Eleven for directions on exchange of papers and student evaluation. If you did not require the students to write out their plans of attack before writing, have them do so now before the evaluation. The plan of attack should be written on the same paper as the paragraph, either before the paragraph or after the paragraph, depending upon when you assigned this part of the task. Write the following questions on the board or on a handout:

1. Does the paragraph follow the plan of attack that the writer indicated was used? If no, write what you think the writer did.

2. Is the paragraph orderly in its arrangement of sentences?

3. If no to question 2, rewrite the paragraph, arranging the sentences in an orderly pattern.

4. Are there any sentences of either cause or effect that need further sentence(s) of explanation? Which ones are they?

See the end of Lesson Eleven for your role in the evaluation.

Lesson Sixteen (Using Cause/Effect). Follow directions for Lesson Twelve, working with paragraphs of cause and effect.

Lesson Seventeen (Using Explanation). In this type of paragraph, the #2 sentence sets forth an idea, and the rest of the sentences give details to explain the idea. The paragraph may be in coordinate or subordinate sequence, or in mixed sequence, depending upon the idea to be explained.

The paragraph of explanation may involve itself with:

1. A process (how to do something).

2. An idea or a concept (how it works, what it means).

3. A description of an object.

4. A chronological account of an event.

By now, the hard-and-fast definition of structure will not be necessary, because the students will be able to figure out with you how a certain paragraph **will be** structured **before** it is written—or how it **is** structured **after** it is written.

Have students generate topics and #2 sentences for paragraphs of explanation. Remind them that they must formulate in their minds a plan for the structuring of the paragraph before they begin to write it—physical, chronological, order of importance, and so forth. They are to select one topic or #2 sentence for their individual paragraph of explanation. Since the structuring of the paragraphs will vary greatly, tell your students to number their sentences as they write their paragraphs.

Some suggestions for #2 sentences for paragraphs of explanation are given below. They follow the four types of explanation paragraphs mentioned at the beginning of this lesson.

A. Planting a vegetable garden requires effort and planning. (a process)

B. The generation gap is an interesting [or a nonexistent] phenomenon. (a concept)

C. The teacher's desk is the focal point of this room. (a description)

D. This course has concentrated on preparing me to pass the Writing Competency Test [or to be a competent writer]. (a chronological account)

CHAPTER 4

The Essay

This unit is designed to enable students to write a short essay in which an opinion is stated and supported. It provides a simple step-by-step plan virtually all students can follow. The form is useful for a variety of kinds of school writing, but the unit emphasizes the importance of having the most general ideas of an essay in mind before starting to write. The unit also provides a very tight formula for writing an essay. While such a formula may result in rather mechanical writing, we feel it can also supply remedial writers with the confidence they often lack. As students become more proficient, they should be encouraged to loosen their adherence to the formula. A list of suggested follow-up activities enabling students to do this concludes the unit.

From Paragraph to Essay

Before beginning this chapter, students should have completed Chapter 3 and should be able to recognize and write coordinate, subordinate, and mixed sequence paragraphs. The lessons in this chapter move from paragraph to essay writing. Students will complete three essays during the unit. If they have access to computers, the writing process will be easier.

Lesson One. Introduce the unit by explaining the importance of being able to write a clearly organized essay. Review the concepts of generality, specificity, and subordination from the paragraph unit. Today you will introduce the class to the essay form they will be using, and they will write the introductions to their first essays. Remind them that most paragraphs begin with a highly general #2 sentence that states an idea to be proven by more specific subordinate sentences. Next pass out Worksheet 1 (page 51), and go over the method the class will be using.

The key to our approach to the essay is the **superordinate**, or #1, sentence. This sentence is similar to the thesis statement or main idea of the standard five-paragraph theme, but students will have an easier time understanding the concept if it is explained as a highly general "umbrella" sentence that the rest of the essay proves. This sentence is followed by two #2 sentences, each stating a single reason why the #1 sentence is true. Continue through the worksheet, explaining the purpose and form of the remaining paragraphs. If students are confused by the form, assure them that their first essays will be written over a period of several days with many checks along the way, and that they will catch on as they work.

After explaining the form, prepare your students to write introductions for their first essays. Have students suggest possible #1 sentences about their school. Write the suggestions on the board, while explaining that a good #1 sentence is neither too general nor too specific. Select a single #1 as the topic for the first essay, then let students suggest reasons the #1 is true. Jot these reasons on the board also, but do not state them as complete sentences.

Students now have what they need to begin the introductions to their essays and may begin writing. They will all have the same #1, but they may choose from among the ideas on the board for their #2's. Remind them that they are writing a 1–2–2 coordinate sequence and that both #2's should be reasons why the #1 is true. The introductory paragraphs should be finished by the end of the period.

Lesson Two. Begin by having students form pairs to check yesterday's introductory paragraphs. Emphasize that they should keep their discussion constructive. They should exchange papers, read them, and discuss the following points, which will be listed on the chalkboard:

1. Does the paragraph start with the assigned #1?

2. Are the #2's reasons why the #1 is true?

3. Are the #2's general enough to be discussed in an entire paragraph?

While this is going on, you can troubleshoot and help those having problems.

When the students have finished, prepare them to continue their essays by reviewing the function of the **supporting paragraphs as** outlined on Worksheet 1. Each of the two supporting paragraphs should discuss a **single** #2 sentence. These paragraphs are mixed sequences that may use explanations, reasons, or examples. They may be similar in form to any of the kinds of paragraphs the students wrote in the paragraph unit, but each begins by repeating a #2 sentence from the introduction. Thus, the first #2 in the introduction (#2a on the worksheet) becomes the first sentence of the first supporting paragraph. The second #2 (#2b) becomes the first sentence of the second supporting paragraph. Students write for the remainder of the period with you available to help.

Lesson Three. Students continue writing their supporting paragraphs with you available to help. The two supporting paragraphs should be finished by the end of the period.

Lesson Four. Begin by having students form pairs to check their supporting paragraphs. They should exchange papers, read them, and discuss the following points:

1. Does each supporting paragraph begin by repeating a #2 sentence from the introduction?

2. Do the remaining sentences in each paragraph stay subordinate to the #2 sentence?

3. Do the supporting paragraphs make good use of reasons, explanations, or examples?

When students are finished, prepare them to write **conclusions** to their essays by referring once again to the essay worksheets. Explain that the purpose of the conclusion is to reemphasize the most important points made in the essay. Students should look back through their essays to decide which points they want to repeat. Remind them that the concluding paragraph should be brief and general and that it should restate the #1 idea. It is usually helpful to suggest some stock phrases (such as **in conclusion, to sum up**) to get them started. Students may now write their conclusions, which are due at the end of the period.

Lesson Five. Students have now completed the rough drafts of their essays, and today they will help one another double-check their writing before beginning final drafts. Each student needs the

rough draft and two copies of Worksheet 2 (page 52). Go over the exercise and explain that each rough draft must be read and commented on by two other students. Again, emphasize that the evaluator's comments be constructive. You also spend the period reading and commenting on the rough drafts.

Lesson Six. The final draft of the first essay is due today at the end of the period. Students should use yesterday's exercise comments to be sure their rewritten papers are correct in form and in mechanics. You are available to help and should remind the class of the importance of a final proofreading (either by the writer or someone else) before turning in the finished paper.

Lesson Seven. Today students begin work on their second essays. Rather than using an assigned topic, the class will generate ideas for writing and turn them into #1 sentences. Begin by suggesting some topics to the class. Cars, motorcycles, pop music, sports, skateboards, jobs, food, a class, or a teacher all make good starters. Write some of these topics on the board, and let the class add ideas they think are better.

Next review the qualities of a good #1 sentence: (1) it is a complete sentence; (2) it expresses an opinion; and (3) it is neither too general nor too specific. Pick one of the topics and get several suggestions from the class for #1's based on it. Write the suggestions on the board and discuss their merits. The point of this process is to have the class see how to move from "Cars" to "The Pontiac Trans-Am is the finest car ever made." Repeat this activity with a second topic from the list on the board. Now pick a third topic and have students privately write #1's based on it. When finished, have each student read his or her sentence aloud to the class and discuss the problems and virtues of some of them. If time allows, repeat this activity also.

The class should now be ready to start writing their essays. They may use the #1's they have written privately or choose a topic from the list on the board and write another #1. Remind them that their #2's should be reasons their #1's are true and that since they may use only two #2's, it is a good idea to think of several and then pick the two best. (You may even want to require a list of four or five #2's from which they may choose before they start writing.) The class may spend the rest of the period writing.

Homework: Students should come to class tomorrow with completed rough drafts of their introductions.

Lesson Eight. This is an ideal time to return the class's first essays with your comments on them. Read several good examples aloud. Quickly review the 1–2–2 form, using Worksheet 1 if necessary. Students may have the bulk of the period to continue their essays, but you should check all introductions as early in the period as possible to be sure all students are proceeding successfully.

Lesson Nine. Students complete the rough drafts of their essays under your supervision.

Lesson Ten. The class should have completed their rough drafts today. Students receive two copies of Worksheet 3 (page 53). Go over the exercise and explain that, as with the first essay, each student's rough draft will be read and commented on by two other students. You, too, will spend the period reading and commenting on rough drafts.

Lesson Eleven. Essays are due at the end of the period. Students may use the period to rewrite their rough drafts, using comments from yesterday's exercise to improve form and content. Remind students to give their papers a final proofreading.

Lesson Twelve. Today students will prepare for a test on the 1–2–2 form. Explain that tomorrow they will write an entire essay during class, much as they might on a competency examination or on an essay test in another class. Write a sample topic on the chalkboard. (Several possible topics are included in the Follow-up Activities at the end of this chapter.) Demonstrate that the #1 sentence for an essay can be based on the topic you assign. The topic "Discuss the reasons your community or neighborhood is a good or bad place to live" becomes the #1 sentence "Topeka is an especially exciting place to live." Have the class suggest several alternate #1's for this topic, write them on the board, and discuss them. Next have them privately write an introduction for an essay on this topic. When finished, read several aloud and discuss virtues and problems. Write a second topic on the board and again have them write practice introductions. Read several aloud and discuss them. End the period by writing the following guidelines for an essay test on the board and explaining them:

1. Base your #1 sentence on the topic you are assigned.

2. Think of several #2 sentences and pick the two best to use.

3. Be sure all sentences in your support paragraphs are subordinate to their #2 sentences.

4. Carefully proofread your essay before turning it in.

Students turn in their practice introductions for credit.

Lesson Thirteen. Today students take the essay test on the 1–2–2 form. Review the guidelines for an essay covered at the end of the period yesterday. Give the students a topic and let them write for the period. (Sample topics are provided in the Follow-up Activities.) Remind them to watch the time.

Follow-up Activities

1. Throughout the unit, emphasis has been on keeping the form of the essay as tight as possible. As students become more proficient— possibly as early as the second essay—they may vary the form. Below is a series of variations in an order suggested for their introduction.

   (a) Repeat the #2 ideas in an altered form, rather than copying the sentences exactly as they are in the introduction.

   (b) Add additional #2 ideas and corresponding support paragraphs to discuss the #1 more fully.

   (c) Precede the #1 sentence with something to capture the reader's interest: a bit of description, a brief example, a question the #1 answers.

   (d) Save a new idea for inclusion in the conclusion.

2. Mastering the essay form is best achieved by continued practice. Additional impromptu essays—similar to the test in Lesson Thirteen— may be written as often as once a week. Here are some sample topics.

   (a) Discuss the reasons your community or neighborhood is a good or a bad place to live.

   (b) It has been suggested that all eighteen-year-old men and women be required to serve in our country's armed forces. Discuss why this is or is not a good idea.

   (c) Some people say it is a good idea for high school students to own an automobile. Others disagree. Discuss why high school students should or should not have cars.

(d) Many high schools are divided into several student groups. Discuss why this division is or is not good for a school.

(e) Some people think sports have become too important in our country. Others feel this is not so. Discuss whether you feel sports are overemphasized.

(f) Teenagers today have few problems. Discuss whether you agree or disagree with this statement and explain why.

(g) Discuss whether or not you feel people should be able to buy alcoholic beverages at age eighteen.

(h) Should helmets be required equipment when riding a motorcycle? Decide what you think and explain why.

(i) Discuss whether a job you have done (for pay or not) was a good or a bad experience to have had.

(j) Decide what you think is the best age to allow people to have driver's licenses. Give the reasons for your choice.

Proving a Point

STUDY THIS

The 1–2–2 system is a way of writing an essay that proves a point. Its first paragraph (the introduction) begins with a #1, or **superordinate**, sentence that states the main idea the essay is going to prove. Following this, are two #2 sentences, each stating one reason why the #1 sentence is true.

Each of the two supporting paragraphs begins by repeating one of the #2 sentences. The rest of each of these paragraphs explains the #2 that begins it.

The final paragraph (the conclusion) repeats the main ideas of the essay.

INTRODUCTION

1–2a–2b

Coordinate Sequence

The purpose of the essay is proving the #1, or superordinate, sentence.

SUPPORTING PARAGRAPH

2a and Mixed Sequence

SUPPORTING PARAGRAPH

2b and Mixed Sequence

A #2 from the introduction begins each supporting paragraph. The rest of each paragraph explains the #2.

CONCLUSION

Repeats Main Ideas

The conclusion repeats the main ideas.

Evaluation One

Name of Evaluator _____

ANSWER THESE

Carefully read the paper you have been given and follow the instructions below.

1. Write the #1 (superordinate) sentence below.

2. Write the #2 sentence for the first supporting paragraph below.

   (a) Is this sentence a reason why the #1 is true? If not, why not?

   (b) Below, write any sentence from the paragraph that doesn't explain or prove the #2 sentence.

3. Write the #2 sentence for the **second** supporting paragraph below.

   (a) Is this sentence a reason why the #1 is true? If not, why not?

   (b) Below, write any sentence from the paragraph that doesn't explain or prove the #2 sentence.

4. What are the main ideas of the essay repeated in the conclusion?

5. Reread the essay.
   (a) Circle any misspelled words.
   (b) Correct any errors you find in punctuation.

Evaluation Two

Name of Evaluator _____

ANSWER THESE

Carefully read the paper you have been given and follow the instructions below.

1. Write the #1 (superordinate) sentence below.

2. Answer the following questions about the **first** supporting paragraph.

   (a) Is the #2 sentence a reason why the #1 sentence is true? If not, why not?

   (b) Does the paragraph include any ideas not subordinate to the #2 sentence? If so, what are they?

   (c) What additional idea might be used in the paragraph as an explanation, reason, or example?

3. Answer the following questions about the **second** supporting paragraph.

   (a) Is the #2 sentence a reason why the #1 sentence is true? If not, why not?

   (b) Does the paragraph include any ideas not subordinate to the #2 sentence? If not, why not?

   (c) What additional idea might be used in the paragraph as an explanation, reason, or example?

4. What are the main ideas of the essay repeated in the conclusion?

5. Reread the essay.

   (a) Circle any misspelled words.

   (b) Correct any errors you find in punctuation.

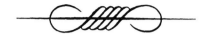

CHAPTER 5

The Letter

One of the most common competencies students must demonstrate for graduation from high school is that of writing letters, especially business letters. Moreover, most students realize that a good deal of the formal writing they will do after graduation is letter writing. This unit teaches students the proper form for both business and personal or "friendly" letters by providing appropriate models and assigning letter-writing problems similar to those they may encounter away from school. The unit takes about two weeks and requires no special materials. However, if students have access to computers, the unit may take less time.

The Business Letter

Lesson One. Introduce the unit by explaining that the business letter form is used for most letters not sent to friends or relatives. The business letter has a standard form that must be adhered to if a letter is to make a good impression and accomplish its purpose.

Copy and pass out Worksheet 1 (page 57), which is a model of the business letter. Better still, project the model on a screen with an overhead projector so the details in form can be pointed out as the model is discussed. First cover the general appearance of the letter: the use of margins; the alignment of the heading, closing, and signature; the skipped lines; and the use of standard-sized white paper. All of this gives the letter a neat, presentable appearance. Next go over the parts of the letter listed here. Give special attention to capitalization, punctuation, and minimal use of abbreviations.

- *Heading.* This consists of the address of the person sending the letter and the date it was written. The heading allows the recipient to be sure of the address to use when responding to the letter. A line should be skipped between the heading address and date and between the date and the inside address.

- *Inside address.* This is the full address of the person or firm to whom the letter is sent. It should include the name and title of the recipient, if known; otherwise the recipient's position or department will do, without a name. A line should be left between the inside address and the salutation.

- *Salutation.* This may take either of two general forms, depending on whether the name of the recipient is known. If the name is known, use Dear Mr. Brown:, Dear Mrs. Brown:, Dear Miss Brown:, or Dear Ms. Brown:. If the name of the recipient is unknown, use Gentlemen:, Gentlepeople:, Dear Sir:, Dear Madam:, or Dear Sir or Madam:. In any case, the salutation is always followed by a colon (:). A line should be skipped between the salutation and the body of the letter.

- *Body.* The body of a business letter is where its business really takes place. Its contents should be clear, brief, and polite. Generally the body of any letters students will write may be divided into two parts: (1) a statement of who the writer is and his or her situation or problem, and (2) a request that the recipient do something. In the model the writer first explains that he is a customer who has ordered a windscreen, then requests that the sales manager expedite delivery. Using this two-part approach to the body gives students a sense of what they should write and neatly divides the letter into two parts that may be treated in two paragraphs. There should be a line between paragraphs of the body and between the body and the closing.

- *Closing.* Any of the following make a simple, polite closing to a business letter: Very truly yours, Cordially, Sincerely, Respectfully. Note that only the first letter is capitalized and that the closing should be followed by a comma.

Several lines should be skipped between the closing and signature.

- *Signature.* The name of the sender is typed or neatly written several lines below the closing. The signature goes between this name and the closing.

After the explanation of the business letter form, the class carefully copies the model letter, being sure to include all appropriate margins, skipped lines, punctuation marks, and capital letters. As students finish their papers, they should bring them to you for a quick check. Students who make serious errors should recopy the letter correctly. Letters are turned in at the end of the period for credit.

Lesson Two. Begin by reviewing the business letter form that was introduced yesterday. Either on their handouts or on yesterday's copied letters, have students circle places where errors are commonly made (for example, commas between cities and states; the colon in the salutation; and the alignment of heading, closing, and signature). The class is now ready to begin its first letter-writing problem. Write the following assignment on the board or pass it out on a handout.

Two months ago you wrote to the subscription department of *Rock It* magazine at 276 West Fifty-seventh Street, New York, New York 10027. You ordered a year's subscription and enclosed a check for twelve dollars, but you have received no response and no magazines. Write a letter explaining the problem and saying what you would like the magazine to do.

Go over this assignment with the class. Stress that a good letter may be written by first explaining the problem, then saying what will correct the problem. The students may work on rough drafts of the letter for the rest of the period. Be available to help as problems arise. Rough drafts should be finished at the end of the period.

Lesson Three. Today students will check their rough drafts in a workshop, then write a final draft. Pass out Worksheet 2 (page 58), which is a business letter checklist, and go over it with the class. The checklist closely follows the business letter model the students already have. Remind the class to have you check their rough drafts after other students read them. Then they may start their final drafts. Be available to help while the class works. Students turn in rough drafts, checklists, and final drafts at the end of the period.

Lesson Four. Today students will complete two drafts of a business letter in a single period. By now they should be familiar with the form, and work should go much more quickly. Put the following letter-writing problem on the board, or pass it out on a handout, and go over it with the class:

Yesterday you received an overdue notice from the Southside Public Library at 1632 Whitney Boulevard in your town. The notice said that you borrowed a book called *The Butterfly Revolution* by William Butler and that the book is now overdue. You know you returned the book three weeks ago—on time. Write a polite letter explaining the error and telling what you would like done to correct it.

Give the class the period to write and rewrite the assigned letter. Suggest that they write the rough draft without looking at the model letter, then check what they have written against the model before rewriting. Inform the class that there will be a test on the business letter tomorrow and that they should review tonight. Give them the period to work. Both rough and final drafts are due at the end of the period.

Lesson Five. Today students have a business-letter test similar to the exercise they did yesterday. Write the following on the board or pass it out on a handout:

Write the principal of this school and tell him or her of a pressing problem facing the school. Explain what you think should be done about it.

Make sure students include the name of the principal and the address of the school. Give the class the period to finish the letter, using two drafts if time allows. Grade each test for appropriate form and content.

The Personal or Friendly Letter

Lesson Six. The second phase of the unit now begins, as students learn the proper form for writing a personal or friendly letter to a friend or relative. Such letters may take the form of a thank-you for a gift or a visit, but more likely they will contain news about recent events in the sender's life.

Copy and pass out Worksheet 3 (page 59), which is a model personal letter, and slowly go over it with the class, pointing out the ways it differs from a business letter. Stress that a personal letter should be conversational, as if one were talking to the person being written to. Remind the class that vague language is dull and that detail and dialogue will do much to add to the recipient's enjoyment of the letter. It is also polite—and makes for a more interesting return letter—if questions are asked of the recipient about what he or she has been up to.

Allow time for questions about the material covered, then give the following assignment:

> Write a letter to a friend (real or imagined) who used to attend this school and has moved away. Tell him or her what has happened to you in the past month. Use proper personal letter form.

Tell the class that personal letters are, by their nature, longer and more detailed than business letters. Then give them the period to write. Rough drafts will be due tomorrow at the start of the period.

Lesson Seven. Having completed the rough drafts of their letters, today students will check their work and start rewriting. As time allows, each student should have either you or another student check the rough draft for mechanics, clarity, and form before beginning a final draft. Rough and final drafts will be turned in tomorrow at the start of the period.

Lesson Eight. Collect both the rough and final drafts of the personal letters to be read and graded. Students will now spend the day learning and practicing the proper way to address a letter for mailing. Pass out Worksheet 4 (page 60), which shows an envelope model, and two copies of Worksheet 5 (page 61) to each student. Go over the envelope form on the worksheet and assign the exercise at the bottom of the page. Doing all six addresses will require both copies of Worksheet 5. While the students work, circulate around the class to help. When students have finshed addressing their envelopes, ask for volunteers to put their work on the board, one envelope per volunteer. Review the work on the board, then have students use it to check their envelopes. Collect the completed work for credit.

Follow-up Activities

Complete mastery and retention of the details of letter-writing form come only with practice. From time to time after completion of the unit, set a class period aside to review the appropriate letter-writing form and assign one of the following problems.

Names, addresses, and other details may be supplied by you or left to the students' imaginations.

Business Letter

1. A clothing store with which you have a charge account has mistakenly billed someone else's purchase to your account. Write a letter explaining the problem and asking for a correction.

2. You are planning a vacation to Mexico. Write the tourist office at the nearest Mexican consulate or at the embassy in Washington, D.C. Ask for information on visas, points of interest, and tourist accommodations.

3. You find a television commercial that is repeatedly shown on a local station very offensive. Write the station explaining why the commercial bothers you and asking for a change.

4. You recently ordered a return-address rubber stamp through the mail. When it arrived, your name was misspelled. Write the company asking for a correction.

5. Write the U.S. Department of the Interior in Washington, D.C., telling them that you are doing a paper on the history and natural environment of some national park. Ask them for help in your research.

6. Write a letter to the editor of a local paper giving your opinion on some current issue.

7. A CD you ordered through the mail has just arrived, but it won't play. Write the company asking them to correct the problem.

Personal Letter

1. Imagine that a relative has just sent you a birthday gift that you have always dreamed of owning. Write a thank-you letter telling the relative how much you appreciate the gift, why you like it so much, and how you will make use of it.

2. Write a letter to a family with whom you spent a weekend not long ago. Thank them for their hospitality and tell them why you had such a good time.

3. Write to a friend who used to live in your neighborhood. Tell him or her about things that have happened or changed since you last saw each other.

Business Letter

1762 Walnut Avenue
St. Louis, Missouri 63141

May 23, 1996

} **Heading**

Sales Manager
Acme Plastics Company, Inc.
934 Sixth Street
Marion, Ohio 43302

} **Inside Address**

Dear Sir or Madam:

Salutation

On April 3, I mailed you an order for a motorcycle windscreen (model 205), enclosing a check for $57.95 to cover the price and shipping costs.

Since I have not yet received the screen and will soon leave on a long motorcycle trip, I would appreciate your looking into the matter and shipping the screen as soon as possible. Your ad promised delivery in four weeks.

} **Body**

Sincerely,

Walter Denning

Closing

Walter Denning

Signature

Business Letter Checklist

Name of Evaluator _____

CHECK THESE Carefully read the paper you have been given. Circle any misspelled words. Then check the letter for the items in the list below. If the item is done correctly, mark a check below. If there is an error, leave the item blank below and circle it in the letter.

Overall Appearance

_____ Standard paper size

_____ Good margin all around

_____ Heading, closing, and signature in line

Heading

_____ Comma between city and state

_____ Comma between date and year

_____ Line skipped between address and date, and between date and inside address

Inside Address

_____ Comma between city and state

_____ Line skipped between inside address and salutation

Salutation

_____ Period after Ms., Mrs., or Mr., if used

_____ Colon (:) used following salutation

_____ Line skipped between salutation and body

Body

_____ All paragraphs indented or all paragraphs unindented

_____ No run-ons or incomplete sentences

_____ Line skipped between paragraphs and between body and closing

Closing

_____ First word only is capitalized

_____ Comma used following closing

_____ Several lines skipped before signature

Signature

_____ Name written out beneath signature

LOOK AGAIN What important details from the problem, if any, are not mentioned in the letter?

Personal Letter

1762 Walnut Avenue
St. Louis, Missouri 63141
April 12, 1996

Dear Ari,

_____

_____

_____

_____

_____

_____

_____

_____

_____

_____

Best,
Prue

Form

A personal letter is similar to a business letter, except for the following:

1. There is no inside address.
2. There is a comma (,) rather than a colon (:) after the salutation.
3. The salutation and closing are more casual.

   Sample salutations: Hi Tommy,
   Greetings from Ohio,

   Sample closings: Your buddy,
   As ever,
   With love,

Content

A personal letter is best if it sounds conversational—as if you were talking to someone. Fill it with detailed news and ask questions of the person you are writing.

The Remedial Writing Teacher's Handbook

Envelope

Oleg Vontoff
134 Hyde Street
Oakland, CA 94602

Mina Clyde
Personnel Office
American Box Company
4362 Third Street
San Francisco, CA 94133

TRY THESE

Carefully study the model envelope above. Then supply proper capitalization, punctuation, and form to the following addresses below as you copy them onto the envelopes on Worksheet 5. Use your own return address.

1. subscription department   auto world magazine
   1734 shattuck avenue   oak hill mi 48015

2. hazel lowe   office of public affairs
   department of transportation   washington dc 20013

3. thomas gishe   far west trucking company
   726 b street   boise id 83701

4. dr mary jennings   oak view medical group
   737 clayton avenue   suite 3   rochester ny 14617

5. manager   honolulu help personnel agency
   671 broad street   honolulu hi 96822

6. milton s lowney   office of admissions
   stockton state university   stockton ca 95202

(continued)

Envelope *(continued)*

PART TWO

Writing Projects

CHAPTER 6

Giving and Following Instructions

This is a two- to three-week unit in giving and following oral and written directions. Its goals are to have students understand that giving clear instructions requires careful thought, and to have them become aware of the audience for whom they write instructions. During the course of the unit, students will write and follow one another's instructions in (1) making a simple drawing, and (2) finding an unknown spot on their school campus. The unit culminates with each student writing a long set of directions for a simple task which must then be demonstrated to the rest of the class. The only unusual materials required for the unit are the designs to be drawn on three-by-five-inch cards for Lessons Two and Three and the list of spots on campus for Lessons Three, Four, and Five. Access to computers for writing the drafts and final paper is helpful.

Drawing a Design

Lesson One. Briefly outline the unit and its goals to the class. Today student volunteers will attempt to give directions to the class for drawing simple geometric designs. Begin by explaining the following terms and writing them on the chalkboard with examples, for reference during the rest of the period: **perpendicular, parallel, right angle.** Next demonstrate the process of giving instructions by giving the class directions for drawing a geometric design they have not seen. (See Examples of Designs for Oral Directions, page 67.) Emphasize two things in the demonstration: (1) the importance of having a plan for the order in which the lines of the design are drawn, and (2) the ease with which the instructions can be understood if each line of the drawing is dealt with in a separate step. The students make drawings according to your instructions. Then the

actual design is drawn on the board so students can check their drawings with the original.

The process may now be repeated several times, with student volunteers giving instructions for drawing additional designs. Mention that giving such instructions is not as easy as it first appears, and help student volunteers by talking with each for a moment about how the drawing will be presented to the class. The period ends with a short discussion of the reasons some directions were better than others. Students turn in their completed drawings for credit.

Lesson Two. Today each student will write a set of directions for drawing a geometric design similar to the ones used in Lesson One. Each student receives a three-by-five card with a design and a number on it. (See Examples of Designs for Written Directions, page 67.) Students should keep the designs they receive a secret. Write the following assignment on the board and go over it with the class:

1. Write your name and the number of your drawing on a piece of paper.

2. Think about your drawing and decide on the simplest order for drawing the lines in it.

3. Write a clear set of directions for drawing your design.

    (a) Write your directions as a series of steps.

    (b) Use a separate step for each line of the design.

    (c) Write in complete sentences.

4. Try your directions on someone who has not seen your design. Improve your directions, rewriting as necessary.

5. Attach a blank sheet of paper to your directions before turning them in with your card.

The blank sheet will provide a place for the comments of students who use the directions tomorrow. Try out as many sets of student directions as possible while writing is going on so you can make suggestions.

Lesson Three. Students are now ready to try out one another's directions for drawing designs. Pass out yesterday's papers, but keep the numbered three-by-five cards on your desk. Write the following assignment on the board and go over it:

1. Exchange your directions with someone else in the class who has not seen your design.

2. Carefully read the directions you receive and attempt the drawing on a piece of scratch paper.

3. Check the drawing you have made with the original, using the number on the directions to find the appropriate card on the teacher's desk.

4. On the blank sheet of paper attached to the directions, answer the following questions:

    (a) What part of the directions was easiest to follow?

    (b) Where did you have trouble?

    (c) In what way could the directions be improved?

    (d) Sign your comments.

The entire lesson hinges on keeping the students from seeing the designs they are trying to draw. Do all you can to keep these a secret until the students check them at the desk.

Homework: At the end of the period, each student receives a slip of paper with a number and a specific spot on campus written on it. The assignment is to find exactly where the place is and to come to class tomorrow prepared to write directions from the classroom to the assigned spot. Some examples: the library card catalogue, the teachers' mailboxes, the soda machine, the door to the principal's office, the trophy showcase. Each slip of paper has a number, and the teacher should keep a master list of locations and numbers.

Finding a Location

Lesson Four. The assignment today is for students to write directions to the places on campus that they have been assigned. Begin by explaining that they should imagine they are writing for a stranger to the school. Thus, they should **describe** landmarks, rather than simply naming them. They should write "Turn right and walk along the locker-lined hallway to the outside exit at the end of the corridor," rather than "Turn right and walk out of the main building." The directions should be written so that the destination is obvious when it is reached. For example, the directions might end: "You are now standing directly in front of your goal."

Write the following assignment on the board and go over it.

1. Be sure you know your goal. Plan a simple route before you start writing.

2. Write your name and the number of your destination at the top of a piece of paper.

3. Write your directions as a series of steps. Each step explains one part of the route.

4. Describe landmarks along the way so someone following your directions will know he or she is not lost.

5. Do not name places or the goal. Describe them.

6. Attach a blank piece of paper to your directions before turning them in.

It is helpful to read a teacher-written set of directions as an example before students start writing. Let them work on their directions in class and be available to head off problems as they arise. Again, as with the designs, secrecy is important, since students will be trying one another's directions tomorrow. Collect directions at the end of the period.

Lesson Five. Today students will try out the directions they wrote yesterday. They will also write comments for the authors of the directions they try. Put the following assignment on the board and go over it:

1. Pick up a set of directions (from the teacher's desk). Follow the directions to their goal.

2. Return to class and check the teacher's master list to be sure you reached the right place.

3. Answer the following questions on the attached blank sheet of paper (for the writer of the directions):

    (a) Did you make it to the goal?

    (b) Were the directions easy or hard to follow? Why?

(c) **What step(s) gave you trouble? Why?**

(d) Sign your comments.

4. Try four or five sets of directions during the period. Make comments on each set you try.

Emphasize the importance of keeping the goals a secret from those trying the directions, and allow most of the period for students to follow directions. Be sure each student is able to read the comments other students have made on his or her paper before it is turned in for credit.

Homework: Students should come to class tomorrow with an idea for a simple task to write directions for and to demonstrate at a later date. Their choices should be specific, limited, and take no more than five minutes to perform. The greatest problem in this assignment is helping students to come up with good ideas. Some examples: sharpening a knife, making popcorn, snapping a football from center, setting the gap on a spark plug, dividing fractions, changing a tire, saddling a horse.

Performing a Task

Lesson Six. Make the assignment for this unit's major project explained on Worksheet 1 (page 68). By this time, students should have a fairly good idea of how to plan a set of directions and how to divide a process into steps for writing. Stress the importance of explaining terms, tools, and equipment to someone unfamiliar with a task being described. Reading a sample paper aloud is helpful, or students can be asked to bring sets of directions from home to discuss.

For some students, the demonstration is a bit more complicated and intimidating than the written directions. Go over the guidelines on Worksheet 1, explaining that the job is to **teach** something to a group of people. Emphasize that an attempt should be made to give the class something to look at (illustrations, equipment, etc.) and, if possible, to get people involved in the task being explained. Having given the assignment, let the class start writing. As they work, confer with students individually about their choices, being sure that they are neither too simple nor too complicated. Let the students know that they will have two more days to finish their rough drafts.

Lessons Seven and Eight. The students work on their written directions in class under your supervision. Rough drafts are due at the start of Lesson Nine.

Lesson Nine. Today is a workshop on the rough drafts of the written directions. Each student receives two copies of Worksheet 2 (page 69). Go over the sheet and explain that each rough draft must be read and commented upon by two other students. You should also spend the period reading and commenting on rough drafts in individual conferences.

Lesson Ten. The final draft of the directions is due today at the end of the period. In rewriting their papers, students should use the suggestions made during the rough draft workshop and by you. Remind the class that demonstrations start tomorrow and that they should review the guidelines for the demonstrations on Worksheet 1. Students should practice their demonstrations at home before presenting them to the class.

Lessons Eleven, Twelve, and Thirteen. Set these days aside for student demonstrations. Expect to get through eight or ten presentations a day. Grading of both written directions and class demonstrations may be based on criteria such as organization, clarity, and difficulty of the process described.

Examples of Designs

For Oral Directions

1
2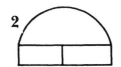
3
4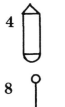

5
6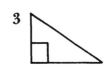
7
8

For Written Directions

1
2
3
4
5

6
7
8
9
10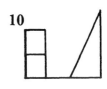

11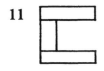
12
13
14
15

16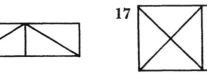
17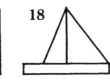
18
19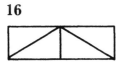
20

21
22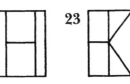
23
24
25

26
27
28
29
30

The Remedial Writing Teacher's Handbook

Assignment

TELL AND SHOW

This week and next, you will be doing two things: (1) writing a clear set of directions for a simple task, and (2) demonstrating the task to the class.

Written Directions

Your directions should be written as **a set of steps** for someone who has never performed the task before. Be sure to explain any terms, equipment, or tools the person reading your directions may not be familiar with. A short introduction (before the steps) is a good place to explain these things. Illustrations may also be included. But your explanation should be mostly in words.

Class Demonstration

You will also demonstrate your task to the class. Bring any necessary equipment, and remember the guidelines below:

1. Plan and practice carefully. The class will not be able to follow your instructions unless you have told them what to do first, what to do second, and so on.

2. Be sure you have explained any terms that someone unfamiliar with your task might not know.

3. Think of an opening and a closing for your talk. The first two or three sentences should capture the class's attention and tell them how many steps to expect. A good way to close is to ask for questions.

4. You may want to get the class involved in doing what you are explaining. You are trying to teach them something, and the best way to teach is to get your learners involved.

5. Your demonstration should be about five minutes long.

Workshop Questions

Name of Evaluator _____

CHECK THESE	Carefully read the paper you have been given. Circle any words you think are misspelled. Correct any errors in punctuation. And answer the following questions.

1. Does the paper have an introduction?

2. Does the paper give instructions as a set of steps?

3. Which unusual terms or tools are not explained well enough?

4. What part of the paper is especially good? Why?

5. Which step or steps in the paper could be clearer? How could that part be improved?

6. If the paper has illustrations, are there any ways in which they could be clearer?

7. If the paper has no illustrations, where could they be added to make the instructions clearer?

CHAPTER 7

Showing vs. Telling

This unit, which lasts about two weeks, teaches students to distinguish between vague writing that merely **tells** and more mature writing that **shows** through the use of lively detail. Students write several short papers and a longer, polished one. The unit is especially valuable if it precedes a more extensive writing project (see Chapters 8 through 11) in which the skills developed here can be reinforced. The only unusual materials required for this unit are the matchbooks for Lesson Four. Access to computers for writing drafts and final papers is a help.

Recognizing Writing That Shows

Lesson One. Introduce the unit by explaining that good writing shows rather than tells. It uses detail that allows a reader to see, hear, and feel what is being described or explained. For the next several days, the class will be working on turning writing that tells into writing that really shows what is going on.

Write the following sentence on the chalkboard:

> The old woman approached.

This sentence **tells** two things: (1) that there was an old woman and (2) that she approached. We have no idea how she looked (Is she happy or depressed? friendly or hostile? well-groomed or disheveled?) and no idea how the approach was made (fast or slowly? with ease or with difficulty?). Underline the words **woman** and **approached** on the board. These are the facts of the sentence that need to be shown to improve the writing. Read the following example of a description that shows the old woman's approach:

> At first she was an ill-formed, dark shape in the distance. As she came nearer, I saw more: the shabby black dress, the unkempt gray hair, the battered purse. She moved slowly, stooped over a twisted walking stick, her stockings in loose wrinkles. Her face was creased and her eyes were set deep into her head.

This passage **shows** the old woman by using detail: her shape, dress, hair, purse, stockings, face, and manner of walking.

Now ask the class to write a similar description of the approach of a different old woman. Give them five or ten minutes to work. (You may want to write an example yourself.) When finished, have several students read their work aloud or read it aloud for them. Point out good details and, perhaps, places where detail could be improved.

Write a second sentence on the board:

> He [or She] left angrily.

Underline the words **left** and **angrily**, explaining that this sentence tells two things that could be shown: (1) a departure and (2) anger. Mention that using dialogue is a particularly good way to show anger, but that there are others (such as facial expressions, body language, silence). Now have the class write passages that show the sentence. An example might be:

> "Then forget it!" Melissa shrieked. She whirled around, headed for the door, and jerked it open.
>
> "Forget it!" she snapped over her shoulder, and the door crashed behind her.

When students have finished writing, read several papers aloud, mentioning virtues and problems of each. Collect written work for credit.

Homework: Write the following sentence on the board:

> The kitchen was a complete mess.

Underline **kitchen** and **mess**, since the class is to show these things in their homework papers. Mention objects in the kitchen that might be part of the mess (sink, cupboards, stove, furniture) and list them under the sentence along with other suggestions from the class. Students should come to class tomorrow with a page of description that shows a messy kitchen.

Lesson Two. Collect the homework and read several papers aloud, discussing successful details. Today's activity is much like yesterday's. Students turn sentences that tell into short descriptions that show. Put this sentence on the chalkboard:

> He [or She] was very dressed up.

Give the students five or ten minutes to write, then have some of them read their descriptions aloud. Repeat the activity twice more, using the following sentences:

> She [He] started the car and drove away.
>
> The countryside was beautiful.

Try to have each student read at least one of his or her descriptions aloud before the end of the period. Collect the written work for credit.

Lesson Three. Take a break from writing today by reading the class a short story rich in descriptive detail. We like to use "There Will Come Soft Rains," a description of a futuristic house from Ray Bradbury's *The Martian Chronicles,* but any good, detail-packed story will do. Assign students the task of jotting down three memorable details as you read: a visual detail; a sound detail; and a smell, taste, or tactile detail. When finished reading, have each student read his or her list and tell why each item was remembered. There will, of course, be duplications; but this only serves to emphasize the impact of some showing details.

Firsthand Observation and Description

Lesson Four. Today students will carefully observe and describe the striking, burning, and blowing out of a common match. Pass out a book of twenty matches to each student in the class and place the following assignment on the board:

1. Strike a match. Watch it carefully. Blow it out. Watch the smoke.

2. Write down a single detail you have observed.

3. Repeat the process with all twenty matches until you have a list of twenty details.

4. Use your observations to write a paragraph describing the lighting, burning, and blowing out of a single match.

Before the class begins, ask each student to remember to use all senses (except taste) to observe. You should also strike several matches and make sample observations in front of the class. Students may now complete the assignment, turning in both the list of observations and the finished description at the end of the period.

Major Paper

Lesson Five. Students are now ready to begin their major papers for this unit. Review the importance of careful observation and detail that shows, then pass out and go over the showing worksheet (page 73). Take time to give students some ideas for developing each topic. Next explain that they are to start with a prewriting activity in which they list things they will show in their papers. Explain the chart and allow the rest of the period for students to complete their prewriting and start their rough drafts. Be available to help. Students keep their charts to use as they write and to turn in later.

Lesson Six. Students continue work on the rough drafts, which are due tomorrow at the start of the period.

Lesson Seven. Today will be a workshop day during which students will help each other improve their rough drafts by eliminating sections that tell rather than show. Write the following instructions on the board and go over them with the class:

A. Exchange papers with another student. Do the following to each other's papers:

1. Read the paper carefully.

2. Underline a place that shows well.

3. Circle a place where the paper tells and could be improved if it showed.

4. Sign the paper at the end of the rough draft.

B. Exchange papers with a second student and repeat steps 1 to 4.

C. Have the teacher check your paper.

D. Start your final draft.

Students work the remainder of the period. Be available to help and to make suggestions about showing.

Lesson Eight. Students complete the final drafts of their papers, incorporating the suggestions made by you and by other students yesterday. At the end of the period, the prewriting charts, rough drafts, and final drafts are due and turned in.

Follow-up Activities

1. The math assignment may be substituted or supplemented by a similar activity with peanuts or candies. Students observe, eat, and write.

2. Continue to mark student papers—in rough and/or final form—for sections that tell when they could more effectively show.

Description of a Place

FOR A START

Your assignment is to describe a place so that your writing **shows** what the place is like. The place may be either real or imaginary. Here are some suggestions:

1. your ideal house	4. the place you go to be alone
2. a crowded bus	5. the place you would like to be right now
3. an unusual room in this school	6. the car you would like to own

TRY THIS

When you have chosen the place you will describe, follow these steps:

1. Take notes on the chart below. If you were in the place you are describing, what would you be seeing, hearing, smelling, tasting, and feeling? Make a list of fifteen or twenty things. Keep the list to use as you write your rough draft and to turn in later.

2. Think about how you will **show** the things you have decided to include in your description. How could you include dialogue?

3. Start your rough draft.

Detail Chart

Things Seen	**Things Heard**	**Things Smelled, Touched, Tasted**

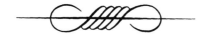

CHAPTER 8

The Memory Project

This project, like that described in Chapter 7, requires students to **show** in their writing, not merely **tell**. It also gives them a chance to experiment with the sentence structures they have combined or modeled in Chapter 2. This project can last from four to nine weeks. Structure your time so that you can use the full quarter, especially if class time is to be used for writing, writing lessons, writing exchange and workshops, and revising for the final paper.

Materials needed: Loosely connected autobiographies such as *Daybreak* by Joan Baez (Avon, 1966); a sample of an ongoing journal; access to computers, if available.

Making a Memory List

Lesson One. Tell students that part of their writing project deals with their ability to remember past events in their lives. To start those memories flowing, have each person begin **listing** memories from his or her life—such as important moments; small but special moments; times of being frightened, proud, embarrassed, anxious; times with a particular person in the family or with a certain friend. This list is only to give students ideas. They are **not** to write out the memory story now.

One way to get the students started is for you to look around the room until you see an object that reminds you of some memory from your life. Tell the students briefly what the memory is. Then, aloud, begin to tell another memory that the first one reminds you of. Continue this loose memory association out loud for the students. Not only will it help them to see what you expect as a memory list, but also it will show them the process of association and give some of them some ideas for their own memory lists.[1]

This day can be very exciting as a class experience, as well as stimulating on an individual writer's level, especially if you participate both in listing memories and in sharing some aloud to spark the memories and the interest of your writers.

Give the students ten minutes to do this listing. Then ask if there are volunteers who will read their lists to the class. Explain that these will serve as catalysts for classmates. Perhaps read your own list, editing where necessary.

Homework: Students are to add to their memory lists so that they have between ten and twenty memories listed by tomorrow.

Lesson Two. Check to see that students have lists of ten to twenty memories. Make notes of those who did not produce enough memories to work with. Tell students that the list is never finished. It may be added to at any time during this project, whenever memories cross their minds. Just because it is on the list, a memory does not have to be selected to be written about. The student has the final choice.

Now it is time to explain the three choices for this autobiography/biography unit. Distribute Worksheet 1 (page 77). Go over it with the students.

Homework: Students are to decide which choice is theirs for the project. Tomorrow they will sign a project commitment sheet. If the choice is A, the writer should extend the existing memory list. If the choice is B, the writer should compile a list of ten to twenty memories with that certain person. If the choice is C, the writer must either buy or staple together a notebook for the original journal, which will be revised and rewritten later.

---

1. This technique is explained more fully by Jim Moffett in *A Student-Centered Language Arts Curriculum: K–13*, pp. 213–214 (Houghton Mifflin Company, 1968).

Writing the Story

Lesson Three. Have students sign the project commitment sheet that you draw up and pass around the class; they are to indicate their choice of project, with those selecting C giving the specific activity they are chronicling.

Explain that class days will be writing workshops and will be used solely for writing out the memory stories, for revising and adding to memory stories and journal entries, and for writing lessons presented by you. Give dates by which each student must have written a certain number of pages (not stories), and explain what quality of writing you expect on those check days.

Today is the first actual writing day on the project. Memory writers must select from their lists one memory to begin writing about. Stress that memory stories will not all be the same length, nor should they be. Show the different lengths of memory stories in *Daybreak*. Some are only one paragraph, while others are seven pages long. This will help students see that they will have the first voice in deciding the length of a memory story. However, if you or a student evaluator feels that more is required for a particular story, usually in the form of description or explanation, then the writer will have to try to expand on a piece.

Tell students to try to begin writing the story as it comes naturally to them, stressing that this is a **first** draft, not a final story. Have them write on every other line, leaving spaces for adding in words and sentences later.

Journal writers should use this day as a time to write the introduction to the journal, in which they explain the nature of the activity that they are involved in. This is the background for the journal. It should reveal both information about the writer and reasons for the individual's involvement in this particular activity or organization.

Homework: Students are to complete the writing they begin in class.

Lesson Four. Check for completed stories. For your own information, note the length of each.

Ask students what is meant by **showing** writing, as opposed to **telling** writing. After you receive a good response, tell them to think of one partner in the class whom they can ask to read their first story and for whom they will do the same. Along with a careful reading, the evaluator should indicate examples of good showing with an asterisk (*) and places where more showing is needed with an X. In the margins,

the reader should also jot down brief questions to help the writer to show better: When? How did this happen? What kind of wagon? What did she wear?

As a model, if possible, write a very brief and sketchy version of one of your memories, without much detail description, or explanation. Ask the students to raise their hands, as you read aloud, when they would like more information or explanation or description about anything. Take about ten minutes to demonstrate, having them ask their margin questions out loud. Then have the class divide into partners and exchange stories to begin looking for good showing and for places where good showing is needed.

Circulate around the class, taking time to read parts of several student papers. Either go in some kind of order or remember whose papers you read so that during a week or so you read some writing by every project writer.

Homework (optional): Tell students to begin another memory story if they have time and want to. The second memory story is due in three days.

Revising

Lesson Five. Today the writing lesson will be on ways to add description that will help those sections that need showing.

Hand out Worksheet 2 (page 78). Go over it in class. Then have each writer find places in his or her first story, the one a partner checked yesterday, to create some sentences like the ones on the worksheet. As changes are made in the stories, tell students to use the lines they skipped to write in new words and new parts of sentences.

Tomorrow you will check the revised memory stories for additions and changes. Mention now that photographs, drawings, or other mementos may be included in this project, so that students can begin to locate these items.

Note: The worksheet contains models followed by places for the students to work on some of their own sentence structures. Example A employs adverb, participial phrase, and dependent adverbial clause. Example B employs adjectives after noun, adjectives before noun, appositive, and dependent adverbial clause plus an adverb. Use this terminology only when and if you feel it is necessary with your particular writers. Emphasize that students should use the commas as they appear in the models.

Lesson Six. Begin by having students work on writing, either on revising or on creating a new memory story. Tell them you are checking for **quality** (of the first memory story of the journal introduction, with revisions, and Worksheet 2, and **quantity** (students should have two to three pages of writing by now). This is a total period of writing. Tomorrow will be an exchange day for the second memory story.

Homework: Students are to complete a second memory story.

Lesson Seven. Follow the same procedures as in Lessons Four and Five. Give Worksheet 2 again to writers who didn't create any or enough of the sentence structures that were presented there. Have them mark the types they did not try so they will try them on this exercise with the second memory story.

Homework: Students are to work on revisions of the second memory story. Work will be checked tomorrow.

Lesson Eight. Check progress while the class works on writing. Read parts as you circulate, pointing out good showing, good sentence structures, and good revisions.

Writing Workshop

Lessons Nine Through Eighteen. Continue using class as a writing workshop. Designate what will be required both in quantity and quality at least two times each week.

Set aside certain days to exchange papers and to look for certain aspects in the writing. Use Worksheets 3 through 5 (pages 79–81) to help with this.

Continue to circulate, reading student papers and offering help in the revision process.

Titles

Lesson Nineteen. Today is Titles Day. Have students create a title for each memory story. This is optional for journal writers. Encourage students to help each other in developing a suitable title for each story.

Table of Contents

Lesson Twenty. Today is Table of Contents Day. Draw a model table of contents on the chalkboard, creating titles from your own memory list or memory stories. Show titles on the left side and beginning page numbers on the right side. Page numbers will be added after the rewriting is completed.

Explain that appearance of the project is **very** important. Remind your students that these papers will combine to make an autobiography, a partial autobiography in journal form, or a story of a relationship with a special person. Therefore, to give a good appearance, the writing project should be placed in some kind of a folder or cover; merely stapling the pages together is not sufficient.

The Final Draft

Lessons Twenty-one Through Twenty-five. Have students use three to five class days for writing final copies. **Before** this final revision and rewriting begins, designate time for paper exchanges for actual proofreading. Student proofreaders are to look for errors in spelling, punctuation, and usage.

Encourage students to ask a parent to proofread also, minimizing the errors for you to discover.

Encourage students to compose their papers on a computer and to print them out.

Evaluation Form

You may distribute Worksheet 6 to students and have them check each other's work. You may also use Worksheet 6 as a guide when grading papers.

Projects

Choose one of the following subjects as a memory-writing project. Be sure to show through precise details what you saw, heard, thought, felt, did, and so on.

A. Memory/Autobiography

Write an autobiography composed of ten or more memories selected from different times in your life. Arrange the memories chronologically. (See *Daybreak*, by Joan Baez, as an example.) Find a title for each memory story. Create a chronological table of contents. Then choose a title for your whole book. Do not attempt to tie the stories together. Instead, let them remain separate memory stories held together by their flow in time.

B. Memories with a Certain Person

This project is very much like the Memory/Autobiography except that all of the stories will revolve around times shared with a certain person. Think of a special relative or a close friend, past or present, whom you would like to focus on in this book. Then make a list of ten to twenty memories of times shared with that person. If you can do that, this may be the project for you. By the way, the finished product makes a lovely gift for the person involved. But be sure to keep a copy for yourself.

C. Journal of an Ongoing Activity

Keep a journal of your involvement in some ongoing activity that you participate in currently and regularly. The activity could be football practice, music lessons, or your after-school job. Make ten to twenty entries in your journal. Polish your writing, just as those working on other projects will polish theirs. Include good descriptions of your thoughts, responses, feelings, and actions.

New Sentence Structures

ASK AND ANSWER Try some of these sentence structures when you are revising your memory or journal entry. Practice the sentence structures on this sheet. Then transfer the new sentence(s) to your paper.

Example: She fell down the stairs.

<u>How</u> did she fall?   She fell down the stairs <u>awkwardly.</u>

<u>Why</u> did she fall?   <u>Not noticing the first step</u>, she fell down the stairs awkwardly.

or

<u>Because she did not notice the first step</u>, she fell down the stairs awkwardly.

TRY THIS

Your Original Sentence: _____

(Questions you need   _____
to answer for readers)   (Revised Sentences)

_____   _____

_____   _____

_____   _____

Example: My grandmother stepped off the plane.

<u>How</u> did she <u>look</u>?   My grandmother, <u>tired but happy</u>, stepped off the plane.

or

<u>Tired but happy</u>, my grandmother stepped off the plane.

<u>Which</u> grandmother?   My grandmother, <u>my mother's mother from Utah</u>, stepped off the plane.

<u>How</u> did she <u>feel</u> or <u>appear</u>?   <u>Although she looked very tired</u>, my grandmother <u>eagerly</u> stepped off the plane.

TRY THIS

Your Original Sentence: _____

(Questions you need   _____
to answer for readers)   (Revised Sentences)

_____   _____

_____   _____

_____   _____

Name _____

Date _____

More Sentence Structures

ASK AND ANSWER | Try some of these sentence structures when you are revising your memory or journal entry. Practice the sentence structures on this sheet. Then transfer the new sentence(s) to your paper..

Example: My uncle led the search party

Can I <u>describe</u> or <u>identify</u> him? | My uncle, <u>who is a veteran Boy Scout</u>, led the search party.

<u>Where</u> did he lead the search? | My uncle, who is a veteran Boy Scout, led the search party <u>down into the canyon</u>.

TRY THIS | *Your Original Sentence:* _____

(Questions you need to answer for readers) | _____

(Revised Sentences)

_____   _____

_____   _____

_____   _____

Example: Elizabeth tried to avoid being hit by the ball.

Can I substitute more <u>vivid</u>, more <u>descriptive</u> verbs? | Elizabeth <u>struggled</u> to <u>escape</u> being <u>smashed</u> by the ball.

TRY THIS | *Your Original Sentence:* _____

(Questions you need to answer for readers) | _____

(Revised Sentences)

_____   _____

_____   _____

_____   _____

Verbs

ASK
AND
ANSWER

<u>Verbs</u> put the <u>action</u> into the sentence. For each action, some of the following questions can be effectively answered by you. The answers can be added to your sentence to make it more descriptive and more real.

How? When? Where? Why?

Example: Tranh read the book.

How?   Tranh read the book <u>quickly</u>.

When?   <u>Yesterday</u> Tranh read the book.

Where?   Tranh read the book <u>under the pear tree</u>.

Why?   <u>Because he loves Indian tales,</u> Tranh read the book.

Combination: Because he loves Indian tales, Tranh read the book quickly yesterday under the pear tree.

TRY
THIS

Write some of your sentences as they now appear in your memory project. Which questions can you answer that would create a better, more descriptive sentence?

1. Original sentence: _____

    Questions: _____

    New sentence: _____

    _____

2. Original sentence: _____

    Questions: _____

    New sentence: _____

    _____

3. Original sentence: _____

    Questions: _____

    New sentence: _____

    _____

Run-ons

WHAT'S WRONG? What is the problem with these sentences?

1. Our vacation was wonderful we toured the West Coast.

2. I'd take any motorcycle you'd give me, my favorite is a Kawasaki.

3. She wrote me a letter last week and she asked me to come visit for a month and she said she would pay the airfare.

(Answer: They're run-ons.)

To Correct a Run-on:

A. Keep the two thoughts as they are expressed and use a semicolon between them. Do this if they are closely related ideas.

   1. Our vacation was wonderful; we toured the West Coast.
      (Notice the lowercase letter after the semicolon.)

B. Use a comma after the first idea, and then add <u>and</u>, <u>but</u>, or <u>or</u> at the beginning of the second idea (if it is appropriate).

   2. I'd take any motorcycle you'd give me, but my favorite is a Kawasaki.

C. Subordinate one of the ideas. Use <u>because</u>, <u>since</u>, <u>however</u>, <u>although</u>.

   2. Although I'd take any motorcycle you'd give me, my favorite is a Kawasaki.

D. Make separate sentences for the ideas.

   3. She wrote me a letter last week, and she asked me to come and visit for a month. She said she would pay the airfare.

TRY THIS Now you write your own run-ons. Then letter A, B, C, or D your method of revising your run-ons. Continue on the back of this sheet if necessary.

1. _____

_____

2. _____

_____

3. _____

_____

_____

Evaluation Form

Name of Evaluator _____

CHECK FOR THESE

Carefully read the paper. Then check the paper, using the following list.

1. Appearance

(a) Type of cover _____

None _____

(b) Method of securing papers

Clamped in folder _____

Stapled _____

Other _____
(Paper clip not acceptable)

(c) Written _____

(d) Typed _____

2. Quantity

(a) _____ handwritten pages

(b) _____ keyboarded pages

3. Sentences

(a) Several run-ons _____

(b) Several fragments _____

(c) Not much variety in sentence structure _____

(d) Good variety in sentence structure _____

4. Description

(a) Good showing description

_____

(b) Not much showing, just telling _____

5. Titles

(a) Titles all there _____

(b) No titles _____

(c) Some titles _____

(d) Clever titles _____

6. Table of Contents

(a) Well done _____

(b) Some problems _____

7. Mechanical Errors

(a) Spelling _____

(b) Punctuation _____

(c) Usage _____

(d) Handwriting _____

8. Extras

(a) Photographs _____

(b) Drawings _____

(c) Other _____

CHAPTER 9

The Biographical Sketch

This writing project performs three major functions. It allows students to express feelings about people close to them, it develops **showing** skills introduced in Chapter 7, and perhaps most importantly, it helps students overcome anxiety about writing a long paper. The unit should be saved for a time when students have confidence in their ability to produce a page or so of writing with ease. By assigning ten short papers and combining them into a single lengthy one (1500 to 2100 words), students produce what for many of them will be the longest paper they have ever written. The project is divided into three stages: (1) a notebook in which information about the subject is gathered; (2) a rough draft that combines the notebook writing into a long, informal biographical essay; and (3) a polished final draft.

The unit is adapted from a project created by Catherine Schengel Townsley and Mary K. Healy of the Bay Area Writing Project of the University of California, Berkeley. It requires no unusual materials, other than a large amount of standard notebook paper (as described in Lesson One). Depending upon other ongoing class activities, the unit takes from four to eight weeks and is easily shortened by reducing the number of assignments in the noteok.

Before Starting the Unit: Several days before starting the unit, take a few minutes during class to talk about selecting a close friend or relative as the subject of a paper to be worked on for several weeks. The subject students choose should be someone they know very well and have seen in a variety of situations. Parents, siblings, and close friends (of the same or opposite sex) make good choices. Subjects should be readily available for an interview that occurs late in the assignment. Students should have several days to choose their subjects and come to class on the day of Lesson One with their selections made.

Notebook Writing

Lesson One. Students will begin the unit by organizing the notebooks in which they will do the preliminary writing assignments for their biographical sketches. Pass out cover sheets for the notebooks, titled "Notebook for Biographical Sketch" (page 87). Have students staple at least twelve sheets of standard binder paper to the cover sheet. Each student writes his or her name and the name of the subject on the cover in the spaces provided. The cover sheet includes an "Assignment Checklist" for each assignment to be completed. Also provided is a space for you to initial each assignment for credit. After explaining the cover sheet, tell the students that each assignment will be about a page long. Have the students write an assignment title, in order, at the top of each blank page of the notebook.

Next describe the biographical sketch in general terms to the class. Each student will be attempting to capture the full range of a subject's personality in writing. The notebook writing assignments are designed to show the subjects in various ways. When the notebook is finished, students will pull most of what they have written into one long descriptive paper. Assure them that the paper will be written slowly, one step at a time, one page per day, and that by the time they have finished their notebooks, it is more likely that they will have too much writing than not enough. Allow time for questions, and check to be sure that all the notebooks have been properly prepared before the end of the period.

Lesson Two. Students are now ready to make their first entry in their notebooks. Ask each student to think of an important memory shared with the subject, a time they both remember fondly. The assignment is to write a minimum of one page describing that memory. Remind students of the important elements of writing that **shows** (see Chapter 7) detail, dialogue, and vivid description. The writing is to be done on the first page of the notebook, headed "Memory #1." Give the class the period to write, and be available to help. At the end of the period, circulate around the room and initial the notebook cover sheets to indicate credit for completion of the assignment.

Lesson Three. Begin the period by asking students to think of an activity (a hobby, a sport, a pastime) or an action (a single event, such as leaving school or swinging a baseball bat) that their subjects regularly perform. The assignment is to describe the subject involved in that activity or action, either alone or with other people. The entry should be made in the notebook on the page headed "Activity or Action #1." Remind the class again of the virtues of writing that shows, and give them the period to work. Be available to help, and read aloud any papers that are particularly successful. Initial notebooks for completion of the assignment at the end of the period.

Lesson Four. In this assignment students will write descriptions of their subjects on the page headed "Physical Description." Start by asking students to name important things they may want to show in their descriptions. List these things on the board. Parts of the face and body, dress, mannerisms, posture, and voice are all characteristics they may want to include. One way to organize such details is to move from head to foot. Another is to show the subject doing something. Give students the period to write, be available to help, and initial notebooks for completion of the assignment at the end of the period.

Lesson Five. This assignment, to be entered on the page headed "Memory #2," is similar to that in Lesson Two. Again students pick an event they shared with their subjects, but they should be careful to choose something that shows a different side of the subject's personality from the one revealed by the event in "Memory #1." Remind students to **show**, give them the period to write, and initial the assignment for completion at the end of the period.

Lesson Six. Since students have chosen subjects they know very well, they should be aware of how their subjects feel about current occupations (whether at school, at home, or in the work world) and about the goals their subjects have for the future. The assignment today, to be entered on the page headed "Feelings About Occupation or Goals," is to write about either or both of these topics. If a student's subject is an adult, the writing can be about the kind of work the subject does, how a typical workday is spent, and how the subject feels about his or her job. If the subject is a high school student, attitudes toward school, teachers, particular classes, or an after-school job can be covered. In either case, the student can write about the subject's goals in life, his or her values, and what the subject would like to be doing in five, ten, or twenty years. Remind the class again about showing, give them the period to work, and initial assignments for completion at the end of the period.

Lesson Seven. Today students have a brief break from the daily writing assignments and will rework an entry they have already done. Ask them to read over the five entries already completed and pick one they think needs work. Write the following on the board while the students go over their work:

A. Exchange the entry you have chosen with another student. Do the following to each other's papers:

   1. Read the entry carefully.

   2. Underline any places in the paper that show well.

   3. Circle any places in the paper that tell and would be more effective if they showed.

   4. Sign the paper.

B. Exchange papers with a second student and repeat steps 1 through 4.

C. Rewrite the entry on a separate piece of paper and add it to your notebook, properly headed.

Go over the assignment on the board and give the class the period to work. Emphasize that this is an opportunity to improve a part of the notebook, and that students should take full advantage of it. Be available to help and to make suggestions as to how papers may be improved. Check for completion at the end of the period.

Lesson Eight. Begin the period by having students open their notebooks to the page headed "Likes and Dislikes" and have them draw a horizontal line halfway down the page. In the space above the line, each student should describe a single thing that the subject likes very much, explain why, and tell how it affects the subject's life. In the space below the line, the same should be done for a single thing the subject dislikes strongly. The topics of these two short pieces may be anything (people, objects, places, ideas). Give the students the period to work. Initial their notebooks to indicate that assignments are complete at the end of the period.

Lesson Nine. The next assignment asks students to record a typical conversation between themselves and their subjects on the page headed "A Typical Conversation." This paper should consist of a discussion students have had many times with their subjects. It could be a debate as to what is a fair time to be home from a date, a talk about which football team is superior, or commiseration about some common problem. The conversation should have only two speakers, the writer and the subject. Ideally it should reveal something about the relationship between them. This may also be a good time to cover the rules for punctuating and paragraphing dialogue (see Worksheet 3 in Chapter 10, page 95). Give the students the period to write, and initial notebooks to indicate completed assignments.

Lesson Ten. This assignment is similar to the one in Lesson Three. Again students describe their subjects involved in a frequently performed activity or action. The subject may be alone or with others, but the activity should demonstrate something new about the subject's personality. Remind the class of the importance of showing and give them the period to write, entering the assignment on the notebook page headed "Activity or Action #2." Initial the notebooks as assignments are completed.

Lesson Eleven. Today students will do a final paper on a shared experience, entering it on the page headed "Memory #3." This time ask them to choose an experience that was unpleasant and encourage them again to try to show a new side of their subject's personality. Let them write for the period, and initial the notebooks as assignments are completed.

Interviewing

Lesson Twelve. Today students will begin preparing for formal interviews with their subjects by writing questions to be used in the interview. On the page of the notebook headed "Interview Questions," have them begin by writing five questions they feel would reveal important aspects of their own personalities if they were being interviewed by someone else. Tell the class to avoid questions that could be answered yes, no, or in a single word, and give them five or ten minutes to work. You may want to write several questions yourself to use as examples. Next have each student spend several minutes going through the notebook to look for ideas for five questions to ask the subject. Finally, have the students write five additional questions they would simply like to ask their subjects and add them to the list.

When all students have fifteen questions, each student will pick two to read aloud to the rest of the class. Go around the room twice, allowing each student to read one question each time. As the questions are shared, students may add to their own lists any questions they hear and think would be useful. At this point each student should have far more questions than are needed for a good interview. Students should pick the ten they feel will be the most effective with their subject. Initial the notebooks for completion. The class is now ready for the interview assignment.

Homework: Students will interview their subjects. Prepare the class by going over the following pointers for a successful interview. It would be wise to write them on the chalkboard or to pass them out on a handout.

1. Hold the interview with only yourself and your subject present. Be away from all distractions.

2. Use the questions you have selected to cover all the points you want, but do not limit yourself to those questions. If an interesting question occurs to you during the interview, ask it.

3. Use follow-up questions to encourage your subject to go into more detail about interesting things he or she has said. (*Examples*: How did that happen? Can you think of an example of that? How do you feel about that? Why did you do that? Do you have anything more to say about that?)

4. Take notes on your interview, but don't try to take down every word. Write only what is important. Too much writing will make the interview tedious and may even make your subject feel awkward.

The notes for the interview should be recorded on the notebook page headed "Interview." If possible, the interview assignment should be made before a weekend, so that students will have adequate time to talk to their subjects.

Lesson Thirteen. Interview notes are due at the start of the period. Begin by initialing notebooks for completion. Next students make their final entries in their notebooks on the page headed "Your Feelings." Ask the class to look back over everything they have written and think about how they feel about their subjects. Then they are to write a page describing how they feel about their subjects and why. Give them the period to write. Initial the notebooks for credit at the end of the period.

The Rough Draft

Lesson Fourteen. Students are now ready to start planning the rough drafts of their biographical sketches. Remind them, that the long-term assignment is to write a paper that shows all aspects of the subject's personality. With this in mind, they should perform two steps before beginning a rough draft. Pass out Worksheet 1 (page 88) and go over it with the class. Be sure students know they are only to select what they feel is the best of their writing. Let them spend the period working and be available to help them plan and select. Check lists for completion at the end of the period.

Lesson Fifteen. The time has come for students to start writing their rough drafts, and it is an ideal time for a lesson on the use of transitional words. Explain that between the long sections from their notebooks they will need short paragraphs to tie the paper together. Pass out Worksheet 2 (page 89) and go over the information on it, explaining how each transitional word could be used to tie together sections of the papers. Have the students keep the worksheets nearby for reference as they write.

Also be sure to explain to students that there is nothing sacred about what they have written in their notebooks. That writing is merely a first attempt. If an idea for improving what is already written occurs to them, they should definitely use it. Remind students that a rough draft should be the best paper that can be written at this point. Give the class the remainder of the period to start writing their rough drafts. For ease in revising, let them compose their drafts at computers, if available.

Lessons Sixteen, Seventeen, Eighteen, and Nineteen. These days are to be set aside as class work periods, though the actual amount of time needed will vary from class to class. You should be constantly available reading papers or computer screens and giving aid, especially with transitions. If, while helping students with their work, you find a good piece of writing, read it aloud to the class.

Lesson Twenty. Rough drafts are due today. Collect the papers at the end of the period and read them out of class, providing comments in the following areas:

1. The degree to which the sketch shows the variety of the subject's personality.

2. The degree to which the paper has successfully used showing writing.

3. Correctness of usage, spelling, punctuation, etc.

It would be wise to schedule an alternate activity in class between Lessons Twenty and Twenty-one to provide time for you to read the rough drafts thoroughly and to give students a well-deserved break from writing.

The Conference

Lesson Twenty-one. Return rough drafts by holding a short conference with each student as you return his or her paper. This will allow you to explain the parts of each paper that are successful and the parts that need further work. You can also make sure the written comments you have provided are fully understood by your students. While you are conferring, the rest of the class can continue the alternate activity from Lesson Twenty.

The Final Draft

Lessons Twenty-two, Twenty-three, and Twenty-four. Students rewrite their papers in class and for homework, using comments provided by you as a guide. We feel that the final draft of a long paper such as this should be presented as handsomely as possible in its final form. It should be written neatly in ink, or on a computer if practical, and be bound in a manila cover. Though students are hesitant to admit it, they are usually proud to have completed so long a project; and the appearance of the final draft can be a symbol that provides a sense of accomplishment.

Follow-up Activities

1. Allow a day in class for students to read one another's sketches. The papers may be passed around the room and commented on in writing on a blank page attached for the purpose. This activity is most successful if it occurs **before** you comment on the papers and grade them.

2. As an additional assignment, require that the completed paper be read and commented upon by the writer's parent or guardian. It could also be read and commented upon by the paper's subject.

Notebook for Biographical Sketch

Student Name _____

Name of Subject _____

Assignment Checklist
_____ 1. Memory #1
_____ 2. Activity or Action #1
_____ 3. Physical Description
_____ 4. Memory #2
_____ 5. Feelings About Career or Goals
_____ 6. Likes and Dislikes
_____ 7. A Typical Conversation
_____ 8. Activity or Action #2
_____ 9. Memory #3
_____ 10. Interview Questions
_____ 11. Interview
_____ 12. Your Feelings

Name _____

Date _____

Planning Your Rough Draft

BEFORE YOU START Before beginning to write the rough draft of your Biographical Sketch, complete the two steps below. Decide what sections of your notebook to include, and decide the order to include them.

Step One. Reread your entire notebook and select the parts you want to use in your rough draft. Do this by:

1. Marking the parts you want to use as you read.

2. Trying to choose writing that shows rather than tells.

3. Picking sections of your notebook that show different parts of your subject's personality. Show him or her in different moods and doing different things.

Step Two. Decide on the order in which you will use the parts you have selected. Make a list of the order. As you make your list, keep the following in mind:

1. Start with action or dialogue to get things moving.

2. Include a physical description of your subject early in your paper.

3. End your paper with the feelings you have about your subject.

When you have finished your list, it should look something like this:

Biographical Sketch Planning List

1. A Typical Conversation

2. Physical Description

3. Part of Activity or Action #1

4. Memory #2

5. Dislikes

6. Part of Interview

7. Feelings About Career or Goals

8. Memory #3

9. Part of Interview

10. Your Feelings

         The Remedial Writing Teacher's Handbook

Transitions

USE THESE WORDS

The words below will be helpful as you organize the writing from your notebook into your rough draft.

When you want to start an example or illustration:

She loves fine clothes. <u>For example</u>, her prom dress cost nearly three hundred dollars.

Jim sometimes becomes bored easily. <u>For instance</u>, I remember something that happened last summer.

When you want to contrast one thing with another:

Maria is one of my best friends. <u>However</u>, she sometimes makes me angry by being late.

Jack is a good swimmer. <u>Even so</u>, he has never won a trophy.

I saw her once when I felt awful. <u>Nevertheless</u>, we had a wonderful time.

When you want to add another idea:

Kareem is crazy about his motorcycle. <u>Furthermore</u>, he does all the maintenance on it himself.

Mr. Johnston is an excellent teacher. <u>Moreover</u>, he is very popular with his students.

Everybody likes Tanisha. <u>In addition</u>, she seems to like everyone she meets.

When you want to show that one thing causes another:

Sam isn't very organized. <u>Consequently</u>, he sometimes doesn't seem to know what he is doing.

One time he forgot his wife's birthday. <u>As a result</u>, she was very angry.

Zhi jogs three miles a day. <u>Therefore</u>, she is in good shape.

When you want to summarize or generalize:

That really bothered me. But <u>on the whole</u>, he is a pretty good guy.

He is sensitive, warm, and considerate. <u>In short</u>, I love him.

CHAPTER 10

The Short Story

In this unit students will write a simple one-episode short story with only two characters. Although the writing of fiction is not usually part of a basic writing course, we feel the unit is quite valuable. It reinforces skills learned in **showing** writing (see Chapter 7), gives students a clear understanding of how a plot works, and provides a chance to learn to punctuate and paragraph dialogue correctly. Moreover, it provides students with a welcome break from expository writing.

The unit lasts about two weeks, once students actually start their stories. The only extra materials needed are class sets of several short stories from any anthology appropriate to the reading level of the class being taught.

Four Concepts

Before Starting the Unit. There are four concepts students should understand before they begin the unit.

1. **Protagonist.** This is the character in a short story with whom the reader identifies—the hero or heroine. He or she is the person we want to win in the story's conflict. If written from a first-person point of view, it is often the protagonist who tells the story.

2. **Antagonist.** Strictly speaking, the antagonist is the problem the protagonist faces in the story. It may be a goal to accomplish, a situation that must be overcome, or a personal psychological difficulty; but in the stories the students will write, the antagonist will usually be another person.

3. **Conflict.** This is the battle waged between the protagonist and the antagonist. It is what gives a story a plot, what causes things to happen. Each episode of a story is a stage in the conflict between the protagonist and the antagonist.

4. **Resolution.** This is the point in a story when the reader discovers whether the protagonist or the antagonist will be victorious in their conflict. It marks the end to the conflict and signals the end to a story.

Read several stories to the class on successive days (or if reading skills of the class enable it, have them do the reading) and discuss each concept as it appears in the stories. For homework, have each student pick an episode of a favorite television program and identify each of the preceding concepts in it. Finally, as a quiz or test, ask each student to identify each concept in a story that has been read but not discussed.

When students have mastered all four concepts, they are ready to begin writing.

Lesson One. Begin the period by reviewing the four story concepts (protagonist, antagonist, conflict, resolution). Then explain the unit in general terms. Students are to write a brief short story in which the conflict is resolved in a single episode or scene. Two characters meet, have a disagreement, and somehow end it.

Pass out Worksheet 1 (page 93) and Worksheet 2 (page 94). First go over Worksheet 1. Emphasize the three things the story should show (see (a), (b), and (c) on the sheet) and the use of dialogue. Take time to provide the class with details that might be used to develop the six situations. What might the characters be like? How would each feel? How might the conflict be resolved?

When most of the class has picked a situation to write about, turn to Worksheet 2. This is a prewriting activity to give students ideas before they actually start writing their rough drafts. Students should jot down ideas about the personality and appearance of their protagonist and antagonist, and then the details of the setting. Give the class the remainder of the period to work. Circulate around the room to be sure all students have selected a situation and have begun work on the planning sheet before the end of the period. Worksheet 2 is due at the start of Lesson Two.

Lesson Two. Begin by checking the planning sheets for completion, but allow students to keep the sheets for reference as they write. These will be turned in later with the final draft.

Students are now ready to start their rough drafts. Have them write at computers, if available. Remind the class that their stories will probably consist mostly of **dialogue** between their two characters and that their stories should **show** each of the following:

1. How the characters are different in personality and appearance.

2. Why they disagree.

3. How the disagreement is resolved.

4. What the setting is like.

Encourage the class to use **showing** writing, and give them the period to work. Be available to help.

Lesson Three. Students continue work on the rough drafts of their stories, which should be complete at the end of the period. Again be available to help.

Lesson Four. Today's lesson is in correctly punctuating and paragraphing conversation. Pass out Worksheets 3 and 4 (pages page 95 and page 96). Slowly go over the six rules on Worksheet 3. Point out that each rule is demonstrated in the circled parts of the example sentence(s) beneath it. Allow time for questions, then dictate the following three sentences:

1. "Sally will arrive soon," I said.

2. "How are you?" she asked quietly.

3. "What," he asked, "are you doing?"

When students have finished writing, put the dictated sentences on the board (or have students do it), and let students check their work before going on.

Next go over the directions for Worksheet 4. Be sure students understand that they only need add quotation marks and paragraphing as they copy the passage over. Let the class work and end the period by having them correct their own exercises according to your instructions. This can be done simply by writing out the exercise on an overhead projector as the class works but not turning on the machine until it is time to correct. Collect the exercises for credit.

Lesson Five. Return the exercises on writing dialogue so students can refer to the six rules as they do this lesson. Today students will rework their rough drafts in a workshop before rewriting. Each student should receive two copies of Worksheet 5 (page 97). Write the following instructions on the board and go over them:

A. Exchange papers with another student. Then do the following:

1. Write your name as "evaluator" on the workshop sheet.

2. Read the short story carefully.

3. Circle a section of the story that **tells** and would be better if it **showed.**

4. Mark the paper and answer the questions according to the directions on the workshop sheet.

5. Return the story to its writer and discuss the comments.

B. Exchange papers with a second student and repeat steps 1 through 4.

C. Have the teacher check your paper if you have any questions.

D. Start your final draft, improving your story according to what you have learned in the workshop.

Give the class the period to work and be available to help. Students should keep the workshop question sheets to turn in with their final drafts.

Lesson Six. Students continue rewriting their stories. Final drafts are due at the end of the period along with rough drafts, planning sheets (Worksheet 2), and the workshop sheets (Worksheet 5) done by the writers' fellow students. Also have students add a blank sheet to their stories.

Lesson Seven. Today students will have an opportunity to read one another's finished stories. As students arrive, desks should be arranged in a single large circle, if possible. Write the following directions on the board and go over them:

1. Quietly and carefully read the story you are given.

2. Write a brief note on one of the following topics for the writer of the story. Use the blank sheet of paper.

(a) What did you enjoy about the story? Why?

(b) What did the writer do in the story that you wish you had done better in yours?

(c) How did you like the resolution? Why?

3. Sign the note and pass the story to the person on your right. Wait to receive a paper from the left.

Peer Evaluation

Pass out unmarked stories at random and let the students read and comment upon them. Your task during the period is to keep papers moving so that each is read several times. Allow time at the end of the period for students to read the comments other students have made on their stories, then collect the papers for grading.

Assignment

TELL A TALE

Your assignment is to create two characters. They are to be different from each other. And they have to disagree about something. Their disagreement has to occur at a single time and in a single place. Your story should show:

(a) How the two characters are different.

(b) Why they disagree.

(c) How the conflict between them is resolved.

PICK ONE

You can use mostly dialogue to show these things. But you should also describe the setting, the way the characters speak, and what they do as they talk. Here are the situations from which you may choose:

1. A high school student arrives home very late at night. A parent is waiting up.

2. A teacher holds a conference with a student and accuses him or her of cheating.

3. A high school student has eaten a hamburger and is about to pay for it. Then the student discovers his or her wallet is gone.

4. A young man has just been stopped for speeding by a female highway patrol officer.

5. The manager of a store stops a high school student whom he or she believes is shoplifting.

6. A high school student who expects to be fired at work is called into the boss's office.

 The Remedial Writing Teacher's Handbook

Planning

FILL
IN THE
CHART Use the spaces below to plot your characters' appearance and personality and the scene of their meeting.

Protagonist	Antagonist
Describe the appearance of your protagonist.	Describe the appearance of your antagonist.
Describe your protagonist's personality.	Describe your antagonist's personality.

Setting
Describe the setting in which your story will take place.

Writing Dialogue

STUDY THESE

Here are the basic rules for punctuating and paragraphing a dialogue correctly.

1. Words actually spoken by a character are placed inside quotation marks (" ").

   ["] Good morning, ["] said Tim happily.

2. Each time a sentence with a different speaker is started, a new paragraph is also started.

   → "My name is Frank," he said as he walked up with a broad smile on his face.

   → She replied, "I'm Susan," and she smiled too, her bright eyes twinkling.

3. A quotation (the words actually spoken by a character) begins with a capital letter whether the quotation comes at the start of a sentence or not.

   "Ⓨou're home early, " remarked Cathy.

   Norman replied, "Ⓦe ran out of money."

4. If a single sentence is quoted in two parts, **two** sets of quotation marks are used, but only **one** capital letter.

   ["] Ǒur business, ["] he said, ["]is better than ever.["]

5. Words that tell who spoke (like **he said** or **Sue announced**) are separated from the quotation by commas. These commas come **before** the quotation marks, never after.

   "Sammy," she said, "is missing again."

   "Wherever I go," Tom said, "he goes too."

6. If a quotation at the beginning of a sentence ends with an exclamation mark (!) or a question mark (?), that punctuation mark replaces the comma before the words that tell who spoke.

   "What's wrong with Ted?" asked Mr. Pine.

   "Run!" we heard him shout.

TRY THIS

Write the dictated sentences.

1. _____

2. _____

3. _____

Writing More Dialogue

MAKE IT RIGHT

The following sentences (adapted from Lewis Carroll's *Alice's Adventures in Wonderland*) are correct except for quotation marks and paragraphing. Copy them in the space at the bottom of the page, adding all missing quotation marks and paragraphing.

Who are you? the caterpillar asked Alice. Alice replied rather shyly, I hardly know, sir, just at present. What do you mean by that? said the caterpillar sternly. Explain your- self. I can't explain myself, I'm afraid, said Alice, because I'm not myself, you see. I don't see, said the caterpillar. I'm afraid I can't put it more clearly, replied Alice very politely, for I can't understand it myself. Being so many different sizes in a day is very confusing. It isn't, said the caterpillar. Well, perhaps you haven't found it so yet, said Alice, but when you have to turn into a chrysalis and then into a butterfly, I should think you'll feel strange, won't you? Not a bit, said the caterpillar.

_____

_____

_____

_____

_____

_____

_____

_____

_____

_____

_____

_____

_____

_____

_____

_____

_____

Workshop Questions

Name of Evaluator _____

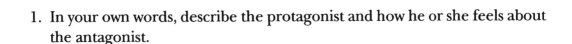

| MARK WITH CARE |

Carefully read the rough draft of the short story. Review the dialogue rules in Worksheet 3. Then circle any errors you find in the paper. Mark any places that need paragraphs with the paragraph mark ¶. Write "No ¶" anywhere an unnecessary paragraph has been included. Then respond to the following.

1. In your own words, describe the protagonist and how he or she feels about the antagonist.

2. In your own words, describe the antagonist and how he or she feels about the protagonist.

3. How is the conflict between the two characters resolved? Who "wins" and why?

Chapter 11

The Research/Interview Project

This project requires writers to go beyond themselves, their memories, and their acquired knowledge. After selecting a topic of real interest, each student will decide which people, places, and kinds of publications can provide helpful information on that topic. This is not a term paper. It is a step-by-step research and interview and writing project that will impress even the writer when it is finished.

This unit is designed to last from four to six weeks. Probably six weeks will be required for remedial writers, who will be doing much of the writing for the project during class time.

The following materials and resources are recommended:

- people to interview
- cooperative and resourceful librarian
- books and computer resources in library
- plain paper or stationery
- cassette tape recorders and tapes
- possible permission to leave campus for interview during school hours
- *An Oral History Primer*, by Gary L. Shumway and William G. Hartley (Box 11894, Salt Lake City, UT 84147)
- computers/word processors

Choosing and Narrowing the Topic

Lesson One. Tell students that for the next unit of study they are going to tackle a type of research paper. The topic for the paper must be something of real interest to them. (It need *not* be a history topic or a geography topic, as many of the students will automatically assume from their previous research experiences.) Tell them to look over Worksheet 1 (page 103) as you go over the requirements with them.

Here are sample topics that some tenth and eleventh graders have chosen to research:

My Family's Russian Heritage

My Family Tree

Surfing on the West Coast

The Status of the Draft in the United States

Rebuilding an Engine for My Car

How to Replace Disc Brakes

A Career as a Butcher

A Career in Clothing Design

Law Enforcement in This City

Multiple Sclerosis: What Is It? How Can I Help Someone with M.S.?

Homework: Tell the students that by tomorrow they are to think of something they are really interested in and want to know more about. They are to be ready to write their topics on a sign-up sheet and to begin Steps 1 through 5 on Worksheet 1.

Lesson Two. Pass a project sign-up sheet around. As it circulates, you should circulate also, finding out which students need to narrow their topics further. For example, if a student has chosen "Surfing" as a topic, explain that people have written entire books on surfing. The topic needs to be more defined, more specific, such as "Surfing Techniques" or "Surfing in California: Where and How." You can involve the students in this discussion, asking for their help in narrowing down some of the topics. Your approval of these limited topics is required as the first step toward success.

Tell students to list on a piece of paper ten or more questions they would like to find answers to about their topics. These questions will form the basis for their beginning research, although they will think of more questions as they work. Tell them to continue to add questions to their question sheet—and remind them to save every bit of writing, note taking, and interviewing that they do.

Homework: Students are to complete ten or more questions about their limited topics by tomorrow.

Library Resources

Lesson Three. If you have a cooperative and resourceful librarian who has time to help with classroom projects, give him or her a list of students' limited topics, along with a request for names of useful publications, and possible places to write, and computer for information for each topic. If no librarian is available to help, either have an advanced student from another class or a student aide do the legwork for you—or do it yourself. These ideas will be needed next week.

Check for the ten questions. As you are walking around, have the students work in pairs to hear each other's questions and to suggest other questions.

Today students will work on Step 2 of Worksheet 1, thinking of names or titles of people and their organizations to whom they will write business letters requesting information about their topics. Again, students may work in pairs with you walking around helping individuals, checking their progress as you go.

Planning the Interview

Lesson Four. Today students will begin to think about the interviews they will conduct as a part of their research papers. Explain that you will be teaching them how to conduct an interview before they actually go out to meet someone. This lesson is the preliminary step. First have students write an opening statement explaining what they are working on and what part the interview plays in constructing this project. They are then to write the name(s) and/or the title(s) of the specific person(s) with whom they will try to set up an interview.

> *Not Acceptable:* A grocery store butcher
>
> *Acceptable:* The head butcher or manager of butchers at Safeway on Main Street

Beneath the names or titles, have the students write the questions from Step 1 (Worksheet 1) that they feel this person will be able to answer or to help answer. After leaving a space on the paper, tell them to try to construct more specific interview questions that will enable them to have their original questions answered.

Homework: Students are to complete the preliminary interview introduction and questions.

Lesson Five. Check for completed preliminary interview introduction and questions. While you are circulating, have students write on a sheet of paper the questions from Step 1 (Worksheet 1) that they expect to find answers to in a publication of some kind. Explain that a question in Step 1 may be included on both the interview sheet and the publication sheet. Then have students write what kind of a publication they will look for, being as specific as possible.

> **Question:** Where can you go to school in this area to learn fashion design?
>
> *Not Acceptable:* Pamphlets from schools
>
> *Acceptable:* Yellow pages of telephone directory
> Books and pamphlets in career section of library
> A vocational school directory

Students will need help figuring out what to look for. You can do this with some of the students orally, using the board to write down their ideas.

Arrange for a day in the library. Ask the librarian to talk with each student about publications and places to write for information.

Library Visit

Lessons Six and Seven. Take the class to the library. Their primary task is to find out where to write for or access information and which sources to look in for information. Take two days if necessary to accomplish this.

The Business Letter

Lesson Eight. Explain to the students that the business letters requesting specific information need to be written and mailed very soon so that responses will be received in time to help with the project. Students are to write at least two business letters to request information. Hand out Worksheet 2 (page 104) and Exercise 1 (page 109) and have students begin one business letter in class, following the directions on the worksheet and the exercise.

Homework: Students are to complete a draft of the first business letter. They are to have a parent or adult proofread the letter, looking for organization and content required by Worksheet 2 and Exercise 1, good sentences, correct spelling, and good punctuation. They are to bring the original, rough draft of the letter with corrections on it to class tomorrow. They are also to bring plain paper or stationery and two envelopes if the school cannot supply them.

Lesson Nine. Have students write their second business letter in class on a computer, if possible, following the directions on Worksheet 2 and Exercise 1. As they write, confer with individual students at your desk, going over the first business letter and its corrections, suggesting any necessary changes.

Homework: Students who have had a conference about the first letter should key and print out or write a perfect copy on plain, unlined paper. Students who have not had the conference should finish the first draft of the second letter. They are to follow Lesson Eight's directions.

Tell students to make interview appointments during the next three days for the week after next. Preparation for the interview will take place in class on the day of Lesson Seventeen. Change it to an earlier day if you need to. Have students submit to you in writing the names and titles of their interviewees, places of interviews, and times of interviews. Make necessary arrangements for those students who need to be excused from classes for an appointment. Keep a record of this information so you can give credit.

Lessons Ten and Eleven. Continue conferences with individuals about business letters, noting progress of each student. Students will be at different stages in their two business letters, and conferences with you will help them tie these stages together. For some students, you will have only one conference, those being the conferees after the first day. Remind students that a copy of each business letter must be included in the project.

Lesson Twelve. Using Exercise 2 (page 110), have students address the two envelopes for their two letters. Credit each student with a finished envelope before it is mailed.

Note Taking

Lesson Thirteen. Today's lesson focuses on note taking in the library. Using the board and Worksheet 3 (page 105), show students the differences between:
  A. a summary
  B. a paraphrase
  C. a direct quote
Explain that you will teach them three different kinds of note taking and that they must decide which will be most useful for each source in the library.

Homework: Have students complete Exercise 3 (page 111).

Preliminary Bibliography

Lessons Fourteen Through Sixteen. Explain that a research paper requires a complete **bibliography**, or alphabetical listing of all the sources used on the paper, at the end. Tell the students to use Exercise 4 (page 112) to write the necessary information for all books, magazines, pamphlets, films, CD-ROM's, and other computer-accessed sources that they will use on the project. A lesson on actually writing the bibliography in its correct format will come later.

Remind the students to take notes on the source on a paper with the question from Step 1 or 5 of Worksheet 1 written at the top of the page. Also tell them to write title and author on the page after each entry. If they are using an encyclopedia, they must write the volume number.

Take students to the library for the remainder of the period and for the next two or three days.

Practice Interviews

Lesson Seventeen. Today will be a preparation day for the interview. Have the students take out the preliminary work they did in Lesson Four—the names or titles of the interviewees, the question from Step 1 (Worksheet 1), and the more specific questions they plan to ask the interviewee. The students who are working on a family tree may have to conduct a telephone interview. The booklet *An Oral History Primer*, by Gary L. Shumway and William Hartley, can be an especially helpful guide to those who are interviewing an older person. Family tree researchers must do more than list the names of ancestors; they must write anecdotes and stories to give life to those characters. They can also research the community the family members came from.

Explain the difference between an **open-ended** question and a **closed** question. The former calls for a fairly broad answer and the answerer has some leeway in choice of response. The closed question requires a specific, very limited answer.

Example:

Closed Question—What was the main determining factor in your becoming an interior designer?

Open Question—What led you to a career in interior decorating?

Have students look over their early questions to see if any are closed. Give them about ten minutes to revise these into more open-ended questions. There are times when a closed question is what they want to ask, but they must realize that an interview full of closed questions would be very stiff and uncomfortable for the interviewee.

For the remainder of the class have students select partners for a practice interview to be given tomorrow.

Homework: Tell students to think of a particular topic to interview a partner about in class tomorrow— an area of interest to that person, a phase of his or her life, something about this individual the interviewer would like to know more about. Students should write ten questions on the topic, mostly open-ended ones. Question papers should have room for notes about the answers, although many students may choose to use a cassette recorder. If so, they should bring the recorder and a tape to class. Some sample topics are: your car, the different schools you have attended, what you want out of your senior year, your family, your job.

Lesson Eighteen. Today students and their partners will interview each other on the specific topic they have selected. Allow fifteen to twenty minutes. If possible, allow students to leave class to sit in halls or outside for their interviews.

Have cassette recorders available for those students who want to use them but were unable to provide their own. The recorder will allow the interview to flow more smoothly than note taking will. (First, brief students about the importance of checking out equipment ahead of time and of using the equipment effectively during the interview.)

When students return to class, have them go over their notes or play their tapes back and make notes. Have them pick out the best parts of the interviews.

Lesson Nineteen. Tell students that yesterday's interview was a trial run. If you have time, use today's class to have students transcribe the best portions of the interview onto paper or on the computer— either from their notes or from their tapes. Printed questions and handwritten answers, or questions typed in capitals, will make an effective interview format. Showing your students a portion of a magazine interview as a model is most helpful at this stage of transcribing.

If you elect not to develop this practice interview further, then use this day to discuss interviewing style and techniques. With **student help** in arriving at

them, list certain guidelines for the interview on the board. Some suggestions:

1. Try to establish a comfortable tone for the interview by being pleasant and informative when you introduce yourself to the interviewee.

2. Explain the interviewee's role in your research project, and present him or her with a permission form. [Worksheet 4, page 106. Students should use one form for each interview they have arranged.]

3. If you are using a tape recorder, set it up and try it out with your introduction to the interview.

4. Try to ask open-ended questions, not closed ones.

5. Avoid interruptions. Instead, write notes to yourself of questions you'd like to ask when your interviewee stops talking.

6. Listen for cues of other questions to ask, ones you hadn't thought of before.
   • Tell me more.
   • Anything happen to show that?
   • Why do you feel that way?
   • What more do you want to say?
   • How did that happen?

7. Listen very carefully to avoid asking a question the interviewee has already included in another response.

8. When the interviewee seems to be finished, ask if there is any more information he or she would like to add.

9. Thank the interviewee for his or her time and cooperation. Tell all interviewees you will send them a copy of the interview. (Then be sure that you do.)

Final Bibliography

Lesson Twenty. The final part of the research paper is the complete bibliography. Distribute Worksheet 5 (page 107) and have students work on their bibliographies during class with your help. Worksheet 5 and Exercise 4 provide the information they need to compile a bibliography. They are to complete it before class tomorrow.

Homework: Students are to finish the bibliography.

Writing the Paper from Notes

Lessons Twenty-one Through Twenty-six. Student notes from publications are written on sheets of paper beneath a question from Step 1 or 5 (Worksheet 1). If possible, have students work at a computer to fit these parts together, that is, decide on an order. They also need to incorporate the information they acquired from the responses to their business letters into the written paper.

Refer to the worksheet on transitions (page 89) as a useful tool at this time.

Refer to Chapter 4, "The Essay," for a guide to forming the introduction and ordering the main parts of the paper. Students will need help in class to put their research essays together. Allow at least five days of class to help the writers organize their letters, interviews, various sets of questions, and worksheets into the order suggested on Worksheet 1.

The writer's personal response, a sort of summary of or reaction to the findings in this paper, should take up one half to one whole page. In it, students can mention information that surprised them, information they knew or expected to find, and what influence, if any, the findings of the research have exerted on them.

Homework: Students are to complete the response step. They should bring all final, revised papers to class for the table of contents.

Finishing Touches

Lesson Twenty-seven. Today have students write their table of contents in class. They will need all final, revised copies.

Provide a model on the board. Designate the place for pages to be numbered, either bottom right or bottom center of each page. Here is a model contents page:

Videotaping a Performance

Also have the students write their title page. A model is:

Videotaping a Performance (center of page)

Pedro Garcia

Composition II

June 1, 1996 (bottom right)

Evaluation/Peer Review

You may use Worksheet 6 as a guide for peer review or when grading the research/interview projects.

The Project

FIRST STEPS

During this unit you will be working on a major paper. Select a topic in which you are really interested and about which you would like to know more. The hours of research will be yours. So make them count. The following requirements will be the beginning steps of the project. We will work on these this week:

1. The questions you have about the topic; what you wish to discover during your research.

2. The names or titles of people and their organizations to whom you will write business letters requesting information.

3. The names or titles of one or two persons whom you will interview to discover some of your answers.

4. The questions you will ask in your interview (at least ten).

5. The items from Step 1 for which you can find answers in a CD-ROM, book, magazine, pamphlet, or Internet connection.

NOTE

Due dates will be announced for each part of the paper. Progress checks will be made along the way. All notes will be checked. The paper will consist of the following:

Title page

Table of contents

Your questions about your topic

Your business letters (copies or carbons)

Responses to your letters

Preliminary interview questions

Your actual written interview (questions with responses)

Your research findings from written sources

Your personal response, a summary of or reaction to your findings

Bibliography

NOTE

The papers may be handwritten in ink or keyed on a computer and printed out. They are to be secured by a folder. All notes, rough drafts, and worksheets are to be included behind the final copy of the paper if your teacher requests them.

Business Letter Model

STUDY THIS

Look closely at this model of a business letter.

2425 Oak Grove Road
Portland, Oregon 97212

October 29, 1996

Sales Manager
J.R. Microwave Systems
256 Main Street
Northport, New York 11768

Dear Sir or Madam:

I am a high school student preparing a research project on microwave devices in transportation. Please send me information about your radar intercept. A friend of mine saw it advertised in *Car and Driver.*

If you have a pamphlet showing your other products, I would appreciate receiving that as well.

It would be especially helpful if you could send me these materials before November 17, as that is our deadline for completing our research. Thank you very much.

Sincerely,

Sasha Loblitt

Sasha Loblitt

NOTE

Notice these facts about the business letter:

1. The **heading** is written a few spaces from the top on the right third of the letter. Follow the punctuation.

2. The **inside address** is written a few spaces below and to the far left of the heading. The first line should be the name or title of the person to whom you are writing.

3. The **greeting** is to a general person if you do not have a name or a title in the inside address. Notice the **colon**.

4. The **body** of the letter will usually be two or three clear, concise paragraphs. In the business letter you may or may not indent.

5. The **closing** is a few spaces below the last line of the letter and directly under the heading. Capitalize the first word only and ("Sincerely," "Yours truly") and use a comma.

6. Write your **signature** above your printed or typed name.

The Remedial Writing Teacher's Handbook

Note Taking

Always carefully write down the source of information (CD-ROM, Web site, book, pamphlet, etc.) after each note-taking entry. Include the page number.

QUESTION: Who were some of the more adventurous doctors of the Old West?

1. The **summary** is what you write when you want to condense what you have read into only a few sentences. Because you will write the book title and page number, you can always go back to it if you need more details.

   Although Pike's Peak is named for Captain Zebulon Montgomery Pike, who did climb it, the first white man to climb it was Dr. Edwin James of the Long expedition.

   —Doctors of the Old West
   Robert F. Karolevitz, p. 26

2. The **paraphrase** is what you write when you change **each** sentence of a certain section into your own words and take notes sentence by sentence.

   There were some adventurous doctors out west. Dr. Jacob Wyeth went on an Idaho expedition in 1832. Dr. John Robinson traveled with Captain Pike in the Spanish Southwest. Dr. Edwin James of the Long expedition along the Platte River actually was the first white man to climb what was later named Pike's Peak.

   —Doctors of the Old West
   Robert F. Karolevitz, p. 26

3. The **direct quote** is exactly what the author wrote. You write the author's words, using quotation marks before and after (" ") and using three dots (. . .) when you leave out some words or sentences.

   "One of Colorado's loftiest mountains is named for Captain Pike—but the first white man to climb the peak was Dr. Edwin James, who accompanied Maj. Stephen H. Long's expedition along the Platte River in 1820."

   —Doctors of the Old West
   Robert F. Karolevitz, p. 26

Permission Forms

FORM FOR EACH

Have each person you interview complete and return one of these forms.

PERMISSION FORM

_____ grants _____
       (Interviewee)   (Interviewer)

permission to use the contents of this interview in his or her research project

for _____
                          (Name of Class)

at _____
                         (Name of School)

_____
(Date)

_____
(Signature of
Interviewee)

- -

PERMISSION FORM

_____ grants _____
       (Interviewee)   (Interviewer)

permission to use the contents of this interview in his or her research project

for _____
                          (Name of Class)

at _____
                         (Name of School)

_____
(Date)

_____
(Signature of
Interviewee)

Model Bibliography

The bibliography shows which sources you have used in writing your research paper. It must be arranged in alphabetical order using the first letter of the first word in the entry, whether it is a person's last name or a title. Here is how to write the entries for different kinds of sources:

1. **Book with one author**
   Karolevitz, Robert F. *Doctors of the Old West*. New York: Superior Publishing Company, 1967.

2. **Book with two authors** (or more)
   Bennett, Hal, and Mike Samuels, M.D. *The Well Body Book*. New York: Random House, Inc., 1973.

3. **Book with an editor**
   Teyler, Timothy, J., ed. *Altered States of Awareness*. San Francisco: W.H. Freeman and Company, 1954.

4. **Book with one section read by you**
   Wickes, Frances G. *The Inner World of Choice*. Englewood Cliffs, N.J.: Prentice-Hall, Inc., 1963, pp.76–96.

5. **Magazine article with an author**
   Dole, Jeremy H. "Behind the Great Muppet Capers." *Families*, Vol. 11, No. 2 (May 1991), pp. 99–108.

6. **Magazine article with no author given**
   "Teen-Agers and Sex: The Price of Freedom." *Adolescence*, Vol. 16, No. 3 (March 1995), pp. 43–47.

7. **Pamphlet with no author given**
   Revised U.S. Edition of Royal Canadian Air Force's *Exercise Plans for Physical Fitness*. Canada: Simon and Schuster, 1991.

8. **Encyclopedia article with author**
   Cowan, Ian McT. "Mammals," *The New Book of Popular Science*. Danbury, Conn.: Grolier Educational Corp., 1990, Vol. 5, pp. 2–15.

9. **Encyclopedia article with no author given**
   "New Caledonia," *Compton's Encyclopedia*, Chicago: Compton's Learning Company, 1995, Vol. 16, p. 162.

10. **Newspaper article**
    Schwartz, Karen. "MCI, AT&T Discussing Joint Effort." *Portland Press Herald*, February 13, 1996, p. C1.

11. **CD-ROM**
    A Passion for Art. Corbis, 1994.

12. **Other Media**
    CD—Hootie & the Blowfish. *Cracked Rear View*. Atlantic Recording Corporation, 1994.
    Video—*Joy of Gardening: Tomatoes & Salads*. Garden Way, Inc., 1986.

Name _____

Date _____

Project Evaluation Form

Name of Evaluator _____

CHECK THESE   Use the following list to check the research/interview papers.

1. **Notes and rough drafts attached**
   Yes _____
   No _____
   Partial notes _____

2. **Appearance**
   Type of cover _____
   None _____
   Method of securing papers _____
      stapled _____
      clamped in folder _____
      other (explain) _____
      (Paper clip not acceptable) _____
   Written _____
   Typed _____

3. **Quantity**
   Typed pages _____
   Handwritten pages _____

4. **Organization**
   Follows assignment sheet _____
   Does not follow assignment sheet

   _____

5. **Table of contents**
   Well done _____
   Some problems _____
   Poor _____
   Missing _____

6. **Business letters**
   Student letters here _____
   Responses here _____

7. **Interview**
   Preliminary questions _____
   Completed interview _____
   Permission form _____

8. **Research**
   Well done _____
   Inadequate _____

9. **Personal response**
   Included _____
   Missing _____

10. **Bibliography**
    Well done _____
    Some problems _____
    Poor _____
    Missing _____

11. **Mechanical errors**
    Spelling _____
    Punctuation _____
    Usage _____
    Handwriting or typing _____

12. **Comments on specific sections:**

Business Letter

ASK FOR INFO

On this paper or at a computer, write a business letter requesting information that will specifically help you with your research paper.

A. Use your home address and actual date in the heading.

B. Be sure to write the name or title, or both, of the person you wish to receive your letter, not just the organization.

C. The body should consist of the following, in three paragraphs:

1. An explanation of your project.

2. A specific request for information—exactly what you want sent to you or what you want to know.

3. A thank-you for a "prompt reply," since time is a crucial factor.

Business Letter Envelope

STUDY THESE

Follow these rules and study the model envelope.

A. Your **return address** includes your name and address. Follow the punctuation.

B. Put the person's name or title above the organization in the **address**.

C. Keep margins straight in both addresses.

D. Do **not** put a comma between the state and zip code.

Sasha Loblitt
2425 Oak Grove Road
Portland, OR 97212

Sales Manager
J.R. Microwave Systems
256 Main Street
Northport, NY 11768

TRY THIS

Address the envelope below as you actually will address the envelope for your business letter to request information for your project. After the teacher checks this practice envelope, address your actual envelope.

Note Taking

TRY THIS

Take notes on the following paragraph in three different ways: summary, paraphrase, direct quote.

It was gold which brought many doctors westward. They came to California, Cripple Creek and Alder Gulch, lured by the magic of El Dorado. Dr. Levi J. Russell suggested Auraria (after his hometown in Georgia) as an early name for the city which ultimately became Denver. In Montana Dr. Gaylord G. Bissell was elected judge of the miners' court at Alder Gulch, and when the pro-Confederate argonauts wanted to name the gold camp Varina—for the wife of Jefferson Davis—he refused to sign any of the legal papers. Then he suggested Virginia City, which he said was "southern enough to suit any rebel."

—*Doctors of the Old West*
Robert F. Karolevitz, p. 101

1. **Summary**

2. **Paraphrase**

3. **Direct Quote**

Bibliography

LIST IT ALL

Write all of the information that is available for each source you use.

    Title

    Author or editor (on title page of book; put "Ed." if editor)

    Publisher (on title page or back of it)

    City published in

    Date of copyright (on back of title page)

    Volume number

    Issue of magazine (date)

    Pages used

NOTE

Use at least **three** written sources. Two of these must be other than encyclopedias (books, magazines, CD-ROM's).

1.

2.

3.

4.

5.

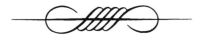

CHAPTER 12

The Poem

Writing poetry can be a very rewarding break in the routine for the remedial writer. By its very nature, poetry is more concise, and this can be a selling point for students who have been producing paragraphs, essays, and even longer writing projects. In addition, poetry need not be entirely separated from prose in the student writer's mind. In writing a poem, the student is exercising an ability to select just the right word. There isn't much room to waste, so each word must be the best choice. Certainly this kind of thinking and evaluating is helpful to a writer of prose as well as poetry.

Expression Follows Experience

Poetry requires the writer to experience something first, then to try to express the idea, feeling, or vision in precisely the right words to convey the message. The writer must **show** in a few words, and they must be the right words.

The kinds of poems presented in this unit are poems that have a formula, precise directions that students of any school age, and certainly high school remedial writers, can follow with guidance. You may wish to supplement the unit by:

Discussing the five senses.

Explaining **imagery**, writing that focuses on the five senses.

Discussing the different sounds of words.

Using vivid and specific words rather than vague and colorless words.

Creating **similes** and **metaphors**.

Sharing poems with your students.

Each type of poem or strategy in this unit is explained on a worksheet; one or more models are given for each. Try to create one poem of each type with the whole class contributing. Write on the board as the students brainstorm and create the poem with you. Be sure they write down the class

creation in their notebooks as a sample before they begin their individual poems on their worksheets.

This unit is designed to last a minimum of one week. The background work that you choose to do, the poems that you collect to share with your students, and the different ways in which you have your students share their poems with each other will determine the actual length of your poetry unit.

Your enthusiasm will be another selling feature—perhaps the main one—for the poetry unit, no matter what depth you choose to go into. If you participate with the class, trying to write each type of poem, your students will be more willing to try a kind of writing many of them feel is foreign to them.

An alternative to a small unit on poetry (and one that a number of writing teachers prefer) is the interspersing of poetry activities and worksheets throughout the writing course.

Poetry Sharing

Here are some possible ways of sharing student poems:

1. Asking for volunteers to read their poems the day after the lesson.

2. Having students come in and write their own poems on the board before class officially begins.

3. Duplicating students' poems (one day their form poems, the next their haiku, etc.) and distributing them to the class.

4. Reading aloud different student poems each day. Be sure to ask the writer's permission to do so.

If you and your students wish to do more with poetry than the scope of this book allows, you may find some of the following materials useful.

A Poetry Resource List

Finn, Louise. *Your Turn: 33 Lessons in Poetry.* Portland, Maine: J. Weston Walch, Publisher, 1988.

Lown, Fredric, and Judith W. Steinbergh. *Reading and Writing Poetry With Teenagers.* Portland, Maine: J. Weston Walch, Publisher, 1996.

Malecka, Janina. *Devices in Poetry and Prose* (18 posters). Portland, Maine: J. Weston Walch, Publisher, 1979

Powell, Brian. *English Through Poetry Writing: A Creative Approach for Schools.* Itasca, Illinois: F.E. Peacock Publishers, 1968.

Stevens, Clark. *"As blue as a rainy day without a friend": Poetry Writing Activities for Middle School.* Portland, Maine: J. Weston Walch, Publisher, 1994.

The Form Poem

IN FOUR LINES

The **form poem** is a four-line poem with alternating lines of four words and three words. These words are not connected so as to make a phrase or a sentence. They are joined only by commas. They may be a mixture of any kinds of words—nouns, verbs, adjectives, adverbs, pronouns, prepositions, interjections. Alternating lines rhyme. And although there is no fixed pattern to the meter, most form poems will have a definite rhythm. Trying them out orally helps to create this rhythm.[1]

* Here is a diagram of the form poem:

_____, _____, _____, _____,   A

_____, _____, _____,   B   (Lines marked A rhyme with each other;
lines marked B rhyme with each other.)

_____, _____, _____, _____,   A

_____, _____, _____.   B

Examples:

<u>German Shepherd</u>

Running, bark, bite, chasing,
   Dodging, jump, power,
Leap, protecting, ours, pacing,
   Smart, playful, tower.

   —Mark Hawkins
     Glenbrook Intermediate School
     Concord, California

<u>Minibikes</u>

Ready, set, go, jump,
   Engines, ouch, crash,
Move, thud, whee, bump,
   What, ah, smash!

   —Darrell Barr
     Glenbrook Intermediate School
     Concord, California

NOTE

The first form poem, "German Shepherd," is a description filled with adjectives, nouns, verbs, and one pronoun to help the reader see the German shepherd. The second one, "Minibikes," is somewhat different in that it is narrative; that is, it tells a story.

(continued)

---

1. We first encountered the form poem in Brian Powell's *English Through Poetry Writing: A Creative Approach for Schools*, pp. 25–28.

 The Remedial Writing Teacher's Handbook

Name _____

Date _____

The Form Poem *(continued)*

TRY THESE

Now write some form poems of your own:

_____
(Title)

_____, _____, _____, _____,

_____, _____, _____,

_____, _____, _____, _____,

_____, _____, _____.

_____

_____, _____, _____, _____,

_____, _____, _____,

_____, _____, _____, _____,

_____, _____, _____.

_____

_____, _____, _____, _____,

_____, _____, _____,

_____, _____, _____, _____,

_____, _____, _____.

The Remedial Writing Teacher's Handbook

Form Poem Variations

THREE FORMS

Here are three examples of form poem variations.

1. An **alliterative** form poem is one in which words begin with the same sound within a line or throughout the poem.

   Example:

   <u>Swimming</u>
   Laughing, lurching, leaping, laps,
   Splish, splash, swim,
   Plummeting, proving, perfect, perhaps,
   Jolly, jackknife, gym.

TRY THIS

Write one of your own:

_____, _____, _____, _____,

_____, _____, _____,

_____, _____, _____, _____,

_____, _____, _____.

2. A form poem that is a **narrative** is one that tells a story.

   Example:

   <u>In My Backyard</u>
   Hummingbird, hovering, honeysuckle, flowers,
   Search, flutter, find,
   Beak, delicate, nectar, ours,
   Nature, sharing, sublime.

TRY THIS

Write one of your own:

_____, _____, _____, _____,

_____, _____, _____,

_____, _____, _____, _____,

_____, _____, _____.

3. A form poem can have a final word that is a surprise or a **punch line**.

   Example:

   <u>True Love</u>
   Love, endless, peaceful, new,
   Spring, hope, dawn,
   Trusting, caring, forever, you,
   Suddenly, empty, gone.

TRY THIS

Write one of your own on the back of this sheet.

The Cinquain (Sĭń-kāne)

The **cinquain** is a five-line poem with definite requirements for each line:

Line 1	One word	What the poem is about (noun).
Line 2	Two words	Words that describe the word in Line 1 (adjectives).
Line 3	Three words	Actions associated with the word in Line 1; what it does (verbs in the same form).
Line 4	Four words	Words that express a thought or feeling about the word in Line 1; words that make a little statement about the word in Line 1.
Line 5	One word	Another word for the word in Line 1; a word that tells how you feel about the word in Line 1 (noun).

Here is a diagram of a cinquain:

_____

_____, _____,

_____, _____, _____,

_____, _____, _____, _____,

_____

Examples:

<u>Wind</u>

Rough, strong
Yelling, howling, destroying
Knocks the trees down
Tornado

<u>Rain</u>

Gentle, cool
Revives, renews, revitalizes
Quencher of thirst
Nectar

—Carson Hackett
John Swett Elementary School
Martinez, California

NOTE 1. The verbs in Line 3 are of the same form. The three in each poem have the same ending.

(continued)

The Cinquain *(continued)*

2. The thoughts in Line 4 are not complete sentences but parts of sentences that make a thought. Avoid "it" structures such as "it knocks down trees" or "it quenches thirst." Also try to avoid intransitive verbs that show no action (am, is, are, was, were, etc.). Look for more expressive and active verbs.

3. The words in Line 5 define the kind of wind (first example), and the writer's feeling about rain (second example).

> **TRY THIS**

Write some cinquains of your own:

_____

_____, _____,

_____, _____, _____,

_____, _____, _____, _____,

_____

_____

_____, _____,

_____, _____, _____,

_____, _____, _____, _____,

_____

_____

_____, _____,

_____, _____, _____,

_____, _____, _____, _____,

_____

Name _____

Date _____

Simile and Metaphor

STUDY THIS

Comparison is a technique that a writer uses often in poetry and in prose. A comparison sharpens the picture presented to the reader. The writer compares the object being described with another that the reader will be able to see clearly, thus forming a better image of the original object.

A **simile** (sih-mill-ee) is a direct comparison of one object to another, using <u>like</u> or <u>as</u>.

A **metaphor** is an implied or indirect comparison of one object with another, in which the one is <u>suggested</u> to have traits or be like the other in some way.

A simile is easy to recognize once you know what to look for:

> And it seems to me you lived your life
> Like a candle in the wind
>
> —Bernie Taupin, "Candle in the Wind," from
> *Goodbye, Yellow Brick Road* by Elton John

TRY THIS

Can you think of some comparisons with <u>like</u> or <u>as</u> in any poems or songs you know? how about in a book you are reading?

A metaphor is not so easy to recognize. But if you think of what is being implied, you'll see it:

> The dandelions nodded their heads in greeting.

Here, the metaphor is created by using a verb not usually used with a certain noun, "The dandelions <u>nodded</u> . . . ." The reader thinks of another subject that usually goes with the verb nod.

Sometimes, although a metaphor is supposed to be implied, the comparison sounds like this:

> All my life's a circle, sunrise and sundown.
>
> —Harry Chapin, "Circle"

This is considered a metaphor because there is no <u>like</u> or <u>as</u>.

TRY THIS

Can you think of any songs or poems that have metaphors in them? how about in a book you are reading? If so, write them on the back of this sheet. Include where you found them.

The Remedial Writing Teacher's Handbook

The Haiku

IN THREE LINES

The **haiku** is a traditional form of Japanese poetry composed of three lines: one of five syllables, one of seven syllables, and one of five syllables. Altogether that is a total of seventeen syllables. The haiku has no other requirements—no complete sentences, no rhythm pattern. The haiku is often used to:

1. capture a moment

2. express a feeling

3. celebrate some phase or element of nature

4. combine several of the above

The haiku is not usually composed of complete sentences, but of pieces of ideas. Therefore, the placement of the words and the use of punctuation can be very important in conveying the message. Avoid hollow, or useless words (**a, an, the**). And avoid intransitive verbs (**am, is, was, were,** etc.) whenever possible in favor of transitive or active ones.

Here are some sample haikus:

Surf pounding like drums,
Sand warm between my brown toes,
My own beach haven.

Dawn through the pear tree,
A lovely way to begin
The joy of summer.

TRY THIS

Write your own haiku here:

_____

_____

_____

The Remedial Writing Teacher's Handbook

PART THREE

Other Competencies

Banking

The forms that go with this chapter are to familiarize students with the banking procedures they will have to follow soon if they are not doing so already.

Included are personal checks, check stubs, deposit slips, withdrawal slips, and an application for credit.

Applications and Forms

The applications and forms included in this chapter are not only useful for the students to become familiar with for general purposes; they are also included in many writing competency tests that we have examined.

Use the forms and applications in class, going over each one with the students as you and the class fill one out together. Then give a blank form or application to each student as follow-up class work or homework. Explain to students that they are to use accurate information about themselves in completing the forms.

Filling out forms is not easy for remedial students. Remember the problem they face in reading and deciphering the words and the chartlike structure of the forms.

Personal Check

STUDY THESE

Here is a sample personal check and a check stub. Study them carefully so that you can complete the following exercise. Sometimes the stub information is in a little booklet attached inside the checkbook.

Check No. *6/7*	**THE BANK** No. *6/7*
Date *8/17/96*	*august 17* , 19*96*
To *Cricket Records*	Pay to the
For *Sonic Boomers*	Order of *Cricket Records* $ *7.42*
Old Balance *112.29*	*Seven and 42/100* Dollars
Deposit *----*	
This Check *7.42*	*Jeanelle Beaulieu*
New Balance *104.87*	
	I: 2100 1020 2I: 58 III 080 III 732II

NOTE

1. Write a check in script. Do not print.

2. Do not erase. If you make a mistake, tear up the check and write a new one.

3. Use ink always, preferably not a felt-tipped pen.

4. Always complete the stub for your own records.

TRY THIS

You are purchasing a new basketball backstop from Big 10 Sporting Goods for $25.71. This is the seventy-first check you have written. Your balance was $127.42. You deposited $100.00 this morning before you shopped.

Check No. _____	**THE BANK** No. _____
Date _____	_____ , 19___
To _____	Pay to the
For _____	Order of _____ $_____
Old Balance _____	_____ Dollars
Deposit _____	
This Check _____	
New Balance _____	_____
	I: 2100 1020 2I: 58 III 080 III 732II

Deposit Slip

STUDY THIS > Here is a sample deposit slip for a savings account. Study it carefully so that you will be able to complete the ones on Worksheet 3. A checking deposit is made on a form that comes with your checkbook and is only slightly different from this form.

SAVINGS DEPOSIT
United Western Bank

	Dollars	Cents
Currency	7	00
Coins	3	72

Marriot
Branch

Mary Ann Jones
Name

92 Courtland Way
Address

Oraga,   Ca   92030
City   State   Zip Code

June 2, 1996
Date

4/5/80
Account No.

Checks *18-23* 1. *15* | 00
92-004 2. *25* | 00
33-117 3. *20* | 00
____ 4. ____ | ____
____ 5. ____ | ____
____ 6. ____ | ____
____ 7. ____ | ____
$ *70* | *72*
Amount

NOTE >

1. List coins and currency (cash) separately in the spaces provided.

2. The check number is the numerator (top number) of the fractions you will find near the upper right corner of every check.

3. Be sure to write your correct savings account number.

(continued)

Deposit Slip *(continued)*

FILL IT OUT

You received some money for your birthday. You want to deposit it in your savings account number 313452 at the Westmore Branch of United Western Bank. Here is a list of your gifts: $10 cash from Aunt Jo, $2.50 in coins from your cousins, a $5.00 check (13-002) from Uncle Bill, and a $10.00 check (90-456) from Aunt Ruby. Fill out the following savings deposit slip.

SAVINGS DEPOSIT—United Western Bank

_____   _____
Branch   Account No.

_____
Name

_____
Address

City   State   Zip Code

_____
Date

	Dollars	Cents
Currency	_____	____
Coins	_____	____
Checks ____ 1. ____		____
____ 2. ____		____
____ 3. ____		____
____ 4. ____		____
	Amount	

TRY THIS

Exercise: Create your own deposit transaction here. Then complete the following for your deposit.

_____ in coin   Account No. _____

_____ in currency

Check–bank number _____ for $_____

Check–bank number _____ for $_____

Check–bank number _____ for $_____

SAVINGS DEPOSIT—United Western Bank

_____   _____
Branch   Account No.

_____
Name

_____
Address

City   State   Zip Code

_____
Date

	Dollars	Cents
Currency	_____	____
Coins	_____	____
Checks ____ 1. ____		____
____ 2. ____		____
____ 3. ____		____
____ 4. ____		____
	Amount	

The Remedial Writing Teacher's Handbook

Withdrawal Slip

STUDY THIS

Here is a sample withdrawal form to remove money from a savings account. Study the form carefully so that you can complete the following exercise.

SAVINGS WITHDRAWAL
Valley Bank

Downtown
Branch

300-29-6501
Account No.

_____
Name

2032 N.W. Seventh St.
Address

$ *150.23*
Amount

Carsonville, NB 68109
City   State   Zip Code

One hundred fifty and 23/100 Dollars

5/13/96
Date

Damian Martinez
Signature

TRY THIS

You would like to remove $250.00 from the Westmore Branch of the United Western Bank. Your account number is 589643.

SAVINGS WITHDRAWAL
United Western Bank

_____
Branch

_____
Account No.

_____
Name

$ _____
Amount

_____
Address

_____ Dollars

_____
City   State   Zip Code

_____
Date

_____
Signature

Name _____

Date _____

Credit Application Form

FILL IT OUT Here is a typical credit application form. Fill it out, using accurate information about yourself.

Valley Bank of California

OFFICE _____

APPLICATION FOR CREDIT (CONSUMER)

---

1 APPLICANT

You may apply for credit in your name, regardless of your sex or marital status. You need not provide information about your spouse unless (A) spouse will be contractually liable for the account or (B) you are relying on community income or spouse's income to repay this account.

Check Preference		Amount Requested	Purpose: ☐ Auto ☐ Boat ☐ Mobile Home					
☐ Separate Account ☐ Joint Account		$	☐ Other (Describe)					
Name (Last) First		Initial	Age	☐ Married ☐ Unmarried ☐ Separated	Ages of Dependents	Social Sec. No.	Driver's License No.	
Street Address ☐ Live with Parents ☐ Rent ☐ Own		City		State	Zip	How Long? Yrs. Mos.		
Home Phone	Previous Address					How Long? Yrs. Mos.		

2 YOUR BANK ACCOUNTS

Financial Institution	Address	Checking Acct. No.
		Savings Acct. No.
Financial Institution	Address	Checking Acct. No.
		Savings Acct. No.

3 YOUR EMPLOYMENT

Employer	Address	How Long?	Position
		How Long in Profession?	
Business Phone	Previous Employer	Address	How Long?

4 YOUR INCOME. You do not have to list income from alimony, child support or maintenance unless you want us to consider it as a basis for repayment of this account.

Gross Monthly Income from Employer			$
Source of Other Income:		☐ Monthly ☐ Annually	$
		☐ Monthly ☐ Annually	

5 INFORMATION ABOUT SPOUSE OR FORMER SPOUSE. You need not fill out this Section unless: (A) You listed income from alimony, child support or maintenance payments in Section 4; *OR* (B) You are relying on community income or your spouse's income to repay this account; *OR* (C) Your spouse will be contractually liable (will sign) for this account.

Name ☐ Spouse ☐ Former Spouse		Address		Home Phone
Employer		Address		Business Phone
Position	How Long	Gross Monthly Income	Social Sec. No.	Driver's License No.

(continued)

Credit Application Form *(continued)*

FILL IT OUT

ASSETS AND LIABILITIES. If section 5 was completed about your spouse, include your spouse's assets and liabilities also. List all payments for alimony, child support, judgments, liens, bankruptcies, etc. whether court ordered or by agreement. If additional space is required, attach a separate schedule. If less than three liabilities listed, provide two other references.

6   Assets and Liabilities are of: ☐ Applicant ☐ Applicant and Spouse Combined

ASSETS (Names, Addresses, Account Numbers)	CASH or MARKET VALUE	LIABILITIES and MONTHLY PAYMENTS (Names, Addresses, Account Numbers)	1	MONTHLY PAYMENT	UNPAID BALANCE
Cash		If renting, monthly rental			
Stocks and Bonds (Number/Description)		Installment Debt			
Life Insurance (Net Cash Value)					
Face Amount $					
SUBTOTAL: LIQUID ASSETS	$				
Auto (Make and Year)		Auto Loans			
Real Estate (from Schedule below)		Mortgages (from Schedule below)			
Net Worth Business Owned (attach Finan. Stmnt.)		Alimony, Child Support			
Furniture		TOTAL MONTHLY PAYMENTS		$	
Other		TOTAL LIABILITIES	B		$
TOTAL ASSETS A	$	NET WORTH (A - B)			$

1   Indicate with (X) in this column and in Real Estate Schedule below any liabilities which will be satisfied by approval of present application.

SCHEDULE OF REAL ESTATE OWNED (If additional properties owned attach separate schedule)

LOCATION and TYPE OF PROPERTY	FINANCED BY	DATE PURCHASED	ORIGINAL COST	PRESENT MARKET VALUE	MONTHLY PAYMENT	1	BALANCE DUE

7   OTHER INFORMATION. Have you ever filed a petition for bankruptcy or compromised debts with your creditors? ☐ Yes ☐ No

Do you have a will? ☐ Yes ☐ No Is your real estate subject to a declaration of homestead? ☐ Yes ☐ No

Are you responsible for other obligations as a co-signer, guarantor, endorser, etc.? ☐ Yes ☐ No   If yes, please give details.

8   AUTOMATIC TRANSFER AUTHORIZATION (Optional)

Please indicate if you elect to transfer funds on the monthly due date in the payment amount from your checking account no. _____ and apply this amount to the credit (loan) account. ☐ Yes ☐ No

9   SIGNATURES (Spouse's or another person's signature is not required if this is to be your separate account)

EACH SIGNER AGREES: I completed this application for credit and certify that statements made above and on the reverse are true and complete. I authorize the Bank to obtain such information as it may require concerning the statements made by me and agree that the application is the Bank's property whether the credit account is granted or not. I also authorize the Bank to provide information arising from this transaction to others.

Applicant's _____ Date _____   Co-Applicant's _____ Date _____
(other than Spouse)
Spouse's _____ Date _____   Co-Applicant has completed a separate application form which
(if this is to be a joint application)   is attached hereto and is a part of this application.

Name _____

Date _____

Job Application Form

FILL IT OUT

AN EQUAL OPPORTUNITY EMPLOYER

PERSONAL HISTORY AND EMPLOYMENT APPLICATION – SALARIED POSITIONS ONLY

QO-1780-C

DATE

OFFICE LOCATION	NUMBER

All qualified applicants will receive consideration for employment without regard to race, sex, religion, color or national origin, and in accordance with the Age Discrimination in Employment Act of 1967 as amended, which prohibits discrimination on the basis of age with respect to individuals who are at least 40 years but less than 70 years of age, with the Vietnam Era Veteran's Readjustment Assistance Act of 1974, and with Section 503 of the Rehabilitation Act of 1973.

GENERAL INFORMATION

PLEASE PRINT NAME IN FULL	FIRST	MIDDLE	LAST

PRINT PERMANENT ADDRESS	STREET	CITY	STATE (AND ZIP CODE)

TELEPHONE NO.	SOCIAL SECURITY NUMBER	ARE YOU 18 YEARS OR OLDER? ☐ YES ☐ NO	ARE YOU UNDER 70 YEARS OF AGE? ☐ YES ☐ NO

ARE YOU IN THIS COUNTRY ON A TEMPORARY VISA? ☐ YES ☐ NO　　ARE YOU LEGALLY ELIGIBLE TO WORK IN THE U.S.? ☐ YES ☐ NO

ARE YOU WILLING TO TRANSFER/RELOCATE? ☐ YES ☐ NO　　HOW WERE YOU REFERRED TO THIS COMPANY?

NAME AND RELATIONSHIP OF RELATIVES EMPLOYED BY THIS COMPANY

HAVE YOU EVER BEEN EMPLOYED BY THIS COMPANY? ☐ YES ☐ NO	WHEN?	WHERE?

EDUCATION

TYPE	NAME AND LOCATION OF SCHOOL	NO. YEARS ATTENDED	DEGREE RECEIVED	MAJOR FIELD
GRAMMAR SCHOOL			X X X X	X X X X
HIGH SCHOOL				
COLLEGE				
GRADUATE EDUCATION				
TRADE, BUSINESS OR CORRESPONDENCE SCHOOL				

ENROLLED IN ANY COURSES NOW? ☐ YES ☐ NO	WHAT COURSES?	HOW MANY NIGHTS A WEEK?	DATE YOU FINISH

OTHER QUALIFICATIONS

WHAT LANGUAGES OTHER THAN ENGLISH DO YOU SPEAK?　READ?　WRITE?

WHAT ABILITIES OR INTERESTS HAVE YOU DEVELOPED OUTSIDE WORK OR SCHOOL IN WHICH THE COMPANY MIGHT BE INTERESTED?

ACTIVITIES (CIVIC, ATHLETIC, FRATERNAL, ETC. EXCLUDE ORGANIZATIONS WHICH INDICATE RACE, RELIGION, COLOR OR NATIONAL ORIGIN OF MEMBERS.)

CAN YOU DRIVE AN AUTOMOBILE? ☐ YES ☐ NO	ARE YOU A LICENSED DRIVER? ☐ YES ☐ NO	WHAT STATE?	HAVE YOU HAD ANY ACCIDENTS IN THE PAST FIVE YEARS? ☐ YES ☐ NO

IF YES, PLEASE EXPLAIN

SPECIAL MILITARY INFORMATION

ARE YOU A U.S. VETERAN WITH A SERVICE-CONNECTED DISABILITY OF 30% OR MORE? ☐ YES ☐ NO

WERE YOU ON ACTIVE DUTY WITH THE U.S. ARMED FORCES FOR MORE THAN 6 MONTHS, ANY PART OF WHICH WAS BETWEEN AUGUST 5, 1964 AND MAY 7, 1975? ☐ YES ☐ NO

(continued)

Job Application Form *(continued)*

FILL IT OUT

FORMER EMPLOYERS
LIST LAST EMPLOYER FIRST AND INCLUDE MILITARY EXPERIENCE IF APPLICABLE

NAME	ADDRESS (INCLUDE ZIP CODE IF KNOWN)				
NAME OF SUPERVISOR	DATE STARTED	DATE LEFT		SALARY OR WAGE	PER
TYPE OF WORK					
REASON FOR LEAVING			PHONE		

NAME	ADDRESS (INCLUDE ZIP CODE IF KNOWN)				
NAME OF SUPERVISOR	DATE STARTED	DATE LEFT		SALARY OR WAGE	PER
TYPE OF WORK					
REASON FOR LEAVING			PHONE		

NAME	ADDRESS (INCLUDE ZIP CODE IF KNOWN)				
NAME OF SUPERVISOR	DATE STARTED	DATE LEFT		SALARY OR WAGE	PER
TYPE OF WORK					
REASON FOR LEAVING			PHONE		

WHICH OF THE ABOVE JOBS DID YOU LIKE BEST? _____

WHY? _____

_____

IF CHOICE IS POSSIBLE, WHAT KIND OF WORK DO YOU DESIRE? _____

_____

_____

It should be understood that in addition to the above, you may be required to furnish a list of personal references other than relatives or former employers. All information will be treated in a confidential manner but it should be understood and agreed that inquiries will be made of references, former employers, educational institutions, etc., for the purpose of verifying and enlarging upon the statements made by you in this application and that misrepresentation can be just cause for separation or refusal of employment. Applicants are cautioned not to disclose any trade secrets or other confidential information from their current or former employers.

SIGNED	DATE

Name _____

Date _____

Social Security Card Application

FILL IT OUT

SOCIAL SECURITY ADMINISTRATION
Application for a Social Security Card

Form Approved
OMB No. 0960-0066

INSTRUCTIONS

- Please read "How To Complete This Form" on page 2.
- Print or type using black or blue ink. DO NOT USE PENCIL.
- After you complete this form, take or mail it along with the required documents to your nearest Social Security office.
- If you are completing this form for someone else, answer the questions as they apply to that person. Then, sign your name in question 16.

1 NAME To Be Shown On Card
FIRST   FULL MIDDLE NAME   LAST

FULL NAME AT BIRTH IF OTHER THAN ABOVE
FIRST   FULL MIDDLE NAME   LAST

OTHER NAMES USED

2 MAILING ADDRESS Do Not Abbreviate
STREET ADDRESS, APT. NO., PO BOX, RURAL ROUTE NO.

CITY   STATE   ZIP CODE

3 CITIZENSHIP (Check One)
☐ U.S. Citizen ☐ Legal Alien Allowed To Work ☐ Legal Alien Not Allowed To Work ☐ Foreign Student Allowed Restricted Employment ☐ Conditionally Legalized Alien Allowed To Work ☐ Other (See Instructions On Page 2)

4 SEX
☐ Male ☐ Female

5 RACE/ETHNIC DESCRIPTION (Check One Only—Voluntary)
☐ Asian, Asian-American Or Pacific Islander ☐ Hispanic ☐ Black (Not Hispanic) ☐ North American Indian Or Alaskan Native ☐ White (Not Hispanic)

6 DATE OF BIRTH
MONTH DAY YEAR

7 PLACE OF BIRTH (Do Not Abbreviate)
CITY   STATE OR FOREIGN COUNTRY   FCI

Office Use Only

8 MOTHER'S MAIDEN NAME
FIRST   FULL MIDDLE NAME   LAST NAME AT HER BIRTH

9 FATHER'S NAME
FIRST   FULL MIDDLE NAME   LAST

10 Has the person in item 1 ever received a Social Security number before?
☐ Yes (If "yes", answer questions 11-13.) ☐ No (If "no", go on to question 14.) ☐ Don't Know (If "don't know", go on to question 14.)

11 Enter the Social Security number previously assigned to the person listed in item 1.
☐☐☐ – ☐☐ – ☐☐☐☐

12 Enter the name shown on the most recent Social Security card issued for the person listed in item 1.

FIRST   MIDDLE   LAST

13 Enter any different date of birth if used on an earlier application for a card.
MONTH   DAY   YEAR

14 TODAY'S DATE ▶ MONTH DAY YEAR   **15 DAYTIME PHONE NUMBER** ▶ ( ) AREA CODE

DELIBERATELY FURNISHING (OR CAUSING TO BE FURNISHED) FALSE INFORMATION ON THIS APPLICATION IS A CRIME PUNISHABLE BY FINE OR IMPRISONMENT, OR BOTH.

16 YOUR SIGNATURE
▶

17 YOUR RELATIONSHIP TO THE PERSON IN ITEM 1 IS:
☐ Self ☐ Natural Or Adoptive Parent ☐ Legal Guardian ☐ Other (Specify)

DO NOT WRITE BELOW THIS LINE (FOR SSA USE ONLY)				
NPN	DOC	NTI	CAN	ITV
PBC	EVI	EVA	EVC	PRA	NWR	DNR	UNIT
EVIDENCE SUBMITTED				SIGNATURE AND TITLE OF EMPLOYEE(S) REVIEWING EVIDENCE AND/OR CONDUCTING INTERVIEW
				DATE
			DCL	DATE

Form SS-5 (9/89) 5/88 edition may be used until supply is exhausted

The Remedial Writing Teacher's Handbook

Withholding Certificate

STUDY THESE You got the job that you applied for. Now your employer wants you to fill out a W-4 Form for income tax purposes. The following terms are necessary for you to know:

- Employee—you; the person who works for a company

- Employer—the company you work for

- Dependents—the people depending on you for support, including yourself

- Withholding Allowance—the amount of money withheld from your pay

Form **W-4** Department of the Treasury Internal Revenue Service	**Employee's Withholding Allowance Certificate** ▶ **For Privacy Act and Paperwork Reduction Act Notice, see reverse.**	OMB No. 1545-0010 **1995**

1	Type or print your first name and middle initial	Last name		2	Your social security number

Home address (number and street or rural route)	3 ☐ Single ☐ Married ☐ Married, but withhold at higher Single rate. **Note:** *If married, but legally separated, or spouse is a nonresident alien, check the Single box.*
City or town, state, and ZIP code	4 If your last name differs from that on your social security card, check here and call 1-800-772-1213 for a new card . . . . . ▶ ☐

5	Total number of allowances you are claiming (from line G above or from the worksheets on page 2 if they apply) .	**5**
6	Additional amount, if any, you want withheld from each paycheck	**6** $
7	I claim exemption from withholding for 1995 and I certify that I meet **BOTH** of the following conditions for exemption:	

- Last year I had a right to a refund of **ALL** Federal income tax withheld because I had **NO** tax liability; **AND**
- This year I expect a refund of **ALL** Federal income tax withheld because I expect to have **NO** tax liability.

If you meet both conditions, enter "EXEMPT" here . . . . ▶ **7**

Under penalties of perjury, I certify that I am entitled to the number of withholding allowances claimed on this certificate or entitled to claim exempt status.

Employee's signature ▶	Date ▶	, 19

8 Employer's name and address (Employer: Complete 8 and 10 only if sending to the IRS)	9 Office code (optional)	10 Employer identification number

Cat. No. 10220Q

(continued)

Withholding Certificate *(continued)*

FILL
IT
OUT

Form W-4 (1995)

Want More Money In Your Paycheck?
If you expect to be able to take the earned income credit for 1995 and a child lives with you, you may be able to have part of the credit added to your take-home pay. For details, get Form W-5 from your employer.

Purpose. Complete Form W-4 so that your employer can withhold the correct amount of Federal income tax from your pay.
Exemption From Withholding. Read line 7 of the certificate below to see if you can claim exempt status. *If exempt, complete line 7; but do not complete lines 5 and 6.* No Federal income tax will be withheld from your pay. Your exemption is good for 1 year only. It expires February 15, 1996.
Note: *You cannot claim exemption from withholding if (1) your income exceeds $650 and includes unearned income (e.g., interest*

and dividends) and (2) another person can claim you as a dependent on their tax return.
Basic Instructions. Employees who are not exempt should complete the Personal Allowances Worksheet. Additional worksheets are provided on page 2 for employees to adjust their withholding allowances based on itemized deductions, adjustments to income, or two-earner/two-job situations. Complete all worksheets that apply to your situation. The worksheets will help you figure the number of withholding allowances you are entitled to claim. However, you may claim fewer allowances than this.
Head of Household. Generally, you may claim head of household filing status on your tax return only if you are unmarried and pay more than 50% of the costs of keeping up a home for yourself and your dependent(s) or other qualifying individuals.
Nonwage Income. If you have a large amount of nonwage income, such as interest or dividends, you should consider making

estimated tax payments using Form 1040-ES. Otherwise, you may find that you owe additional tax at the end of the year.
Two Earners/Two Jobs. If you have a working spouse or more than one job, figure the total number of allowances you are entitled to claim on all jobs using worksheets from only one Form W-4. This total should be divided among all jobs. Your withholding will usually be most accurate when all allowances are claimed on the W-4 filed for the highest paying job and zero allowances are claimed for the others.
Check Your Withholding. After your W-4 takes effect, you can use Pub. 919, Is My Withholding Correct for 1995?, to see how the dollar amount you are having withheld compares to your estimated total annual tax. We recommend you get Pub. 919 especially if you used the Two Earner/Two Job Worksheet and your earnings exceed $150,000 (Single) or $200,000 (Married). Call 1-800-829-3676 to order Pub. 919. Check your telephone directory for the IRS assistance number for further help.

Personal Allowances Worksheet

A   Enter "1" for **yourself** if no one else can claim you as a dependent . . . . A _____

B   Enter "1" if: • You are single and have only one job; or
              • You are married, have only one job, and your spouse does not work; or   . .   **B** _____
              • Your wages from a second job or your spouse's wages (or the total of both) are $1,000 or less.

C   Enter "1" for your **spouse.** But, you may choose to enter -0- if you are married and have either a working spouse or more than one job (this may help you avoid having too little tax withheld) . . . . **C** _____

D   Enter number of **dependents** (other than your spouse or yourself) you will claim on your tax return . . . . . . **D** _____

E   Enter "1" if you will file as **head of household** on your tax return (see conditions under **Head of Household** above) . **E** _____

F   Enter "1" if you have at least $1,500 of **child or dependent care expenses** for which you plan to claim a credit . . **F** _____

G   Add lines A through F and enter total here. Note: This amount may be different from the number of exemptions you claim on your return ▶   **G** _____

For accuracy, do all worksheets that apply.
• If you plan to **itemize or claim adjustments to income** and want to reduce your withholding, see the Deductions and Adjustments Worksheet on page 2.
• If you are **single** and have **more than one job** and your combined earnings from all jobs exceed $30,000 OR if you are **married** and have a **working spouse or more than one job,** and the combined earnings from all jobs exceed $50,000, see the Two-Earner/Two-Job Worksheet on page 2 if you want to avoid having too little tax withheld.
• If **neither** of the above situations applies, **stop here** and enter the number from line G on line 5 of Form W-4 below.

-------------------- **Cut here and give the certificate to your employer. Keep the top portion for your records.** --------------------

Form **W-4**
Department of the Treasury
Internal Revenue Service

Employee's Withholding Allowance Certificate

▶ **For Privacy Act and Paperwork Reduction Act Notice, see reverse.**

OMB No. 1545-0010

1995

1 Type or print your first name and middle initial	Last name	2 Your social security number

Home address (number and street or rural route)

3   ☐ Single   ☐ Married   ☐ Married, but withhold at higher Single rate.
Note: *If married, but legally separated, or spouse is a nonresident alien, check the Single box.*

City or town, state, and ZIP code

4   If your last name differs from that on your social security card, check here and call 1-800-772-1213 for a new card . . . . . ▶ ☐

5   Total number of allowances you are claiming (from line G above or from the worksheets on page 2 if they apply) .   **5** _____

6   Additional amount, if any, you want withheld from each paycheck . . . . **6** | $ _____

7   I claim exemption from withholding for 1995 and I certify that I meet **BOTH** of the following conditions for exemption:
• Last year I had a right to a refund of **ALL** Federal income tax withheld because I had **NO** tax liability; **AND**
• This year I expect a refund of **ALL** Federal income tax withheld because I expect to have **NO** tax liability.
If you meet both conditions, enter "EXEMPT" here . . . . ▶ **7** _____

Under penalties of perjury, I certify that I am entitled to the number of withholding allowances claimed on this certificate or entitled to claim exempt status.

Employee's signature ▶ _____   Date ▶ _____ , 19 _____

8   Employer's name and address (Employer: Complete 8 and 10 only if sending to the IRS) | 9   Office code (optional) | 10   Employer identification number

Cat. No. 10220Q

(continued)

Withholding Certificate *(continued)*

FILL IT OUT

Form W-4 (1995)   Page **2**

Deductions and Adjustments Worksheet

Note: *Use this worksheet only if you plan to itemize deductions or claim adjustments to income on your 1995 tax return.*

1   Enter an estimate of your 1995 itemized deductions. These include qualifying home mortgage interest, charitable contributions, state and local taxes (but not sales taxes), medical expenses in excess of 7.5% of your income, and miscellaneous deductions. (For 1995, you may have to reduce your itemized deductions if your income is over $114,700 ($57,350 if married filing separately). Get Pub. 919 for details.)   **1** $_____

2   Enter: $6,550 if married filing jointly or qualifying widow(er)
            $5,750 if head of household
            $3,900 if single
            $3,275 if married filing separately   . . . . .   **2** $_____

3   **Subtract** line 2 from line 1. If line 2 is greater than line 1, enter -0-   . . . . .   **3** $_____

4   Enter an estimate of your 1995 adjustments to income. These include alimony paid and deductible IRA contributions   **4** $_____

5   **Add** lines 3 and 4 and enter the total   . . . .   **5** $_____

6   Enter an estimate of your 1995 nonwage income (such as dividends or interest)   . . . . .   **6** $_____

7   **Subtract** line 6 from line 5. Enter the result, but not less than -0-   . . . . .   **7** $_____

8   **Divide** the amount on line 7 by $2,500 and enter the result here. Drop any fraction   . . .   **8**   _____

9   Enter the number from Personal Allowances Worksheet, line G, on page 1   . . . . . .   **9**   _____

10 **Add** lines 8 and 9 and enter the total here. If you plan to use the Two-Earner/Two-Job Worksheet, also enter this total on line 1 below. Otherwise, **stop here** and enter this total on Form W-4, line 5, on page 1   . . . .   **10**   _____

Two-Earner/Two-Job Worksheet

Note: *Use this worksheet only if the instructions for line G on page 1 direct you here.*

1   Enter the number from line G on page 1 (or from line 10 above if you used the Deductions and Adjustments Worksheet)   **1**   _____

2   Find the number in **Table 1** below that applies to the **LOWEST** paying job and enter it here   . . . .   **2**   _____

3   If line 1 is **GREATER THAN OR EQUAL TO** line 2, subtract line 2 from line 1. Enter the result here (if zero, enter -0-) and on Form W-4, line 5, on page 1. **DO NOT** use the rest of this worksheet   . . . .   **3**   _____

Note: *If line 1 is **LESS THAN** line 2, enter -0- on Form W-4, line 5, on page 1. Complete lines 4–9 to calculate the additional withholding amount necessary to avoid a year end tax bill.*

4   Enter the number from line 2 of this worksheet   . . . .   **4**   _____

5   Enter the number from line 1 of this worksheet   . . . .   **5**   _____

6   **Subtract** line 5 from line 4   . . . .   **6**   _____

7   Find the amount in **Table 2** below that applies to the **HIGHEST** paying job and enter it here   . . . .   **7** $_____

8   **Multiply** line 7 by line 6 and enter the result here. This is the additional annual withholding amount needed   **8** $_____

9   **Divide** line 8 by the number of pay periods remaining in 1995. (For example, divide by 26 if you are paid every other week and you complete this form in December 1994.) Enter the result here and on Form W-4, line 6, page 1. This is the additional amount to be withheld from each paycheck   . . . .   **9** $_____

Table 1: Two-Earner/Two-Job Worksheet

Married Filing Jointly				All Others	
If wages from **LOWEST** paying job are—	Enter on line 2 above	If wages from **LOWEST** paying job are—	Enter on line 2 above	If wages from **LOWEST** paying job are—	Enter on line 2 above
0 - $3,000	0	39,001 - 50,000	9	0 - $4,000	0
3,001 - 6,000	1	50,001 - 55,000	10	4,001 - 10,000	1
6,001 - 11,000	2	55,001 - 60,000	11	10,001 - 14,000	2
11,001 - 16,000	3	60,001 - 70,000	12	14,001 - 19,000	3
16,001 - 21,000	4	70,001 - 80,000	13	19,001 - 23,000	4
21,001 - 27,000	5	80,001 - 90,000	14	23,001 - 45,000	5
27,001 - 31,000	6	90,001 and over	15	45,001 - 60,000	6
31,001 - 34,000	7			60,001 - 70,000	7
34,001 - 39,000	8			70,001 and over	8

Table 2: Two-Earner/Two-Job Worksheet

Married Filing Jointly		All Others	
If wages from **HIGHEST** paying job are—	Enter on line 7 above	If wages from **HIGHEST** paying job are—	Enter on line 7 above
0 - $50,000	$380	0 - $30,000	$380
50,001 - 100,000	700	30,001 - 60,000	700
100,001 - 130,000	780	60,001 - 110,000	780
130,001 - 230,000	900	110,001 - 230,000	900
230,001 and over	990	230,001 and over	990

 Printed on recycled paper   *U.S. Government Printing Office: 1994 — 375-119*

Change of Address Forms

WHEN YOU MOVE | Your family is planning to move. You want to be sure that all of your mail is delivered to your new address. So you go to the post office to notify the clerks about your move. They give you several forms to complete.

FORM 1: Notice to the post office

- This form ensures that your letters and bills will be forwarded by the post office to your new address.
- Use your current address as your old one.
- Use this one as your new one: 100 Manzanita Avenue
  Miami, FL 33168

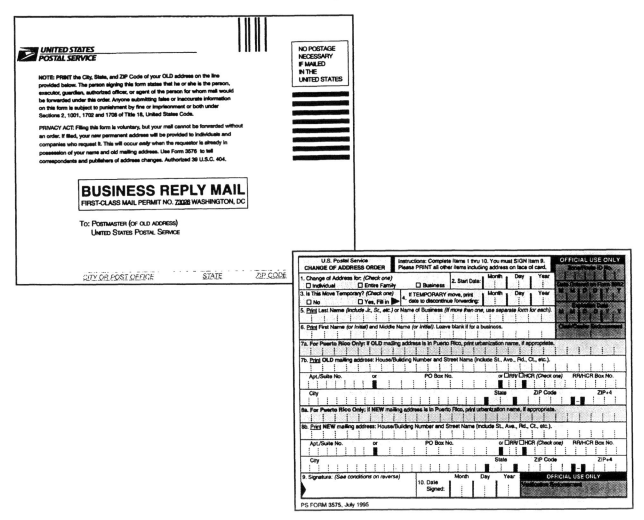

(continued)

Change of Address Forms *(continued)*

WHEN YOU MOVE

FORM 2: **Notice to publishers**

- You would like to continue to receive the magazines and newspapers that you currently receive.
- Fill out the following form, using your current address as the old address.
- The new address is: 100 Manzanita Avenue
  Miami, FL 33168
- The publication is: Scientific Monthly
  314 Pythagoras Lane
  Mansfield, OH 44906

I'M MOVING
PLEASE NOTE MY NEW ADDRESS

Place Stamp Here

TIP: If you need more postcards, every post office has a supply. Ask for "PS Form 3576." Mail will arrive sooner at your new home if it does not have to be forwarded.

ADDITIONAL POSTCARDS ARE AVAILABLE AT YOUR POST OFFICE

Mail this postcard to people and businesses that send you mail.

Name

If Applicable, Name of Business

Complete Street Address or PO Box or Rural Route and RR Box

City or Post Office   State   ZIP or ZIP+4 Code

Mail this postcard to people and businesses that send you mail.

Please send mail to new address beginning: |_|_|_|_|_|
Month Day Year

My Name (Last name, first name, middle initial)

OLD Complete Street Address or PO Box or Rural Route and RR Box   Apt./Suite #

City or Post Office   State   ZIP or ZIP+4 Code

NEW Complete Street Address or PO Box or Rural Route and RR Box   Apt./Suite #

City or Post Office   State   ZIP or ZIP+4 Code

NEW Telephone Number (Optional)

Account Number (If applicable)

Signature   Today's Date: Month Day Year

TIP: Don't forget to inform your family members and friends of your move. It's particularly nice to hear from them when you're settling into a new home.

TELL YOUR FAMILY MEMBERS & FRIENDS 30 DAYS BEFORE YOU MOVE.

The Remedial Writing Teacher's Handbook

CHAPTER 15

The Résumé

Why Write a Résumé?

While writing a résumé is a process usually associated with the completion of work at a college or technical school, it is also a skill included in many competency examinations across the nation. Because of this and because composing a résumé is an excellent way to help students become aware of the marketable skills they have acquired, a short unit in résumé writing is worth including in a remedial writing curriculum. In the lessons that follow, students learn what a résumé is, gather the information needed for résumé writing, and then write two: one of a general nature and one designed for a specific job application. The unit lasts less than two weeks, and the only special materials needed are the help of a school guidance counselor or some newspaper want-ad sections for Lesson Four. The unit is particularly effective toward the end of the academic year when many students are concerned about finding employment—either for the summer or following graduation.

Lesson One. Begin the unit by explaining that a résumé is a formal list of the personal experiences and skills qualifying an applicant for a particular job. Many employers require résumés because they not only give a brief overview of an applicant's education and ability, but also provide an example of the applicant's ability to state information logically and clearly. It is not unusual for employers to request a résumé before granting a job interview. Students will begin by gathering the information they will need to write a successful résumé. Then they will write two résumés—one general and one for a specific job—and a cover letter to accompany a résumé being sent to a prospective employer.

The first step is for students to become aware of the marketable skills they possess and to gather the information they will need to begin writing. Pass out Worksheets 1 and 2 (pages 142–143). These pages are to be filled out as they are explained by you. This process is important, since your purpose is to provide ideas for the résumé that may not have occurred to the students. Students should understand that few of them will have entries in all categories, but that they should think about each so they are aware of **all** their possible work-related experiences. Go over the sheets slowly, one section at a time, using the following steps as a guide:

1. **Name and Address.** Students write their name and address, including zip code and telephone number with area code.

2. **Education.** Students list the names, addresses, and dates of their last four schools. If they do not know the exact addresses of all the schools, the name, town, and state alone will do.

3. **School Skills.** Review with the students the kinds of skills they may have acquired in high school classes. Besides obvious skills learned in business and industrial arts classes, remind them that phys ed, music, and art classes might help in camp and recreation jobs; psychology and child development might help in child care jobs; science in laboratory aide jobs; and knowledge of a foreign language in any job dealing with the public.

4. **Honors and Awards.** Be sure students include any awards or special assignments as teacher aides.

5. **Activities.** Students should include any experience as student-body, class, or club officers and any experience organizing club field trips or fund-raising drives.

6. **Informal Jobs.** This can include almost anything a student has done that involves a job-related skill. Baby-sitting, yard work, housework, painting, or car repairs—to name a few—are tasks a high school student may have

performed that some employers might be interested in.

7. **Formal Work.** This section is for what students might call "real work" for wages from an established firm. If students cannot remember all the names, addresses, and dates they need to complete this section, they may finish it tonight after finding the information they need at home.

8. **Personal.** This section of the sheet allows students to include any additional information about themselves that might be of value. Any travel entries should be designed to show that a student knows something about the world beyond his or her own community. The space for additional skills could include things such as the ability to drive a car, use a computer, or operate a video camera. Be sure students understand that dealing with the public in any job-related capacity can be an important skill.

9. **References.** This section asks students to think of a variety of people whom an employer could contact to verify that an applicant is honest, dependable, and hardworking. Students should understand that it is wise to ask any reference for permission before using the person's name in applying for a job.

10. **Career Goals.** This entry asks students what they want to do as a career following graduation. If a student does not know the educational or training requirements of a chosen career, it is time to find out. A trip to a guidance counselor is suggested in such cases.

The careful completion of the information sheet should take most of the remainder of the period.

Homework: Students who need to find further information to complete their information sheets should do so for homework. The completed sheets are due tomorrow at the start of the period.

Lesson Two. Check the information sheets for completion. Students are now ready to begin the rough draft of a general résumé following a standard form. Remind students that a résumé is designed to give prospective employers a brief summary of skills and not details that would be better covered in a job interview. Therefore, no résumé should be more than one or two typed pages. Pass out Worksheet 3 (page 144), a model résumé, and go over it carefully, pointing out that information about education and

past jobs is always given with the most recent experiences first. Next students should go over their information sheets and mark everything they want to include on their rough drafts. They are now ready to start writing, using the model as a guide. Let them work for the rest of the period while you move about the room to look over their papers. Make sure they are using correct form and including only pertinent information.

Lesson Three. Students complete the rough drafts of their résumés. As each finishes, you should check the work for form and content before the student starts the final draft. As students start rewriting, write the following guidelines on the board and review them with the entire class:

1. To keep the résumé brief, complete sentences are not necessary. Use the model for proper form.

2. The finished résumé should be on standard-sized paper and should be typed if submitted to an employer.

3. Perfect proofreading is essential, since any errors indicate sloppiness and carelessness and create a bad impression of the applicant.

Students continue work. Final drafts are due at the end of the period.

Lesson Four. Having learned a basic résumé form, students may now start work on a résumé to be written with a specific job opening in mind. To start things off realistically, bring help-wanted ads to class for students to look through or have a guidance counselor visit the class to inform students of the kinds of openings available to teenagers.

When either of these activities is completed, have students pick specific jobs for which they feel qualified. Here are some common jobs that might be listed on the chalkboard for students to select from:

1. fast-food restaurant cook
2. file clerk in a small business
3. part-time janitor
4. gas station attendant
5. aide in summer recreation program
6. drugstore sales clerk
7. supermarket bagger
8. door-to-door canvasser
9. coffee shop waiter or waitress
10. nursery school aide

This list should, of course, be altered to conform to the local job market. When students have made their selections, they should consult their information sheets and mark experiences qualifying them for the jobs they have selected. With the job and their own experience in mind, they may start the rough drafts of their résumés and work on them for the remainder of the period.

Lesson Five. Students complete the rough drafts of their résumés and have them checked for form and content by you, but they do not rewrite yet.

Lesson Six. Today, students compose cover letters to accompany their résumés. Those who have a job but no specific employer in mind should either make up an address to use or consult a phone book to come up with a real address. Having done this, they are ready to start the letters. If necessary, review standard business-letter form (Chapter 5). Then write the following assignment on the board and go over it:

Write a letter you could mail to an employer with your résumé. Your letter should include the following:

1. An introduction explaining that you are a high school student looking for work.

2. How you learned about the available job and why you are applying.

3. When you are available to start work.

4. The fact that your résumé is enclosed.

Give the class the period to write and be available to help and to check rough drafts of the letters for form and content. Rough drafts should be complete by the end of the period.

Lesson Seven. Students rewrite the rough drafts of their résumés and letters according to teacher corrections. All work is due in final form at the end of the period.

Follow-up Activities

1. Students actually interested in finding work may mail their letters and résumés to prospective employers.

2. Students rewrite their résumés, emphasizing different skills, for a second kind of job.

3. Students may do interviews and write résumés for friends or relatives.

Résumé Information

FILL IT OUT

Full Name _____ Phone ( )_____

Address _____ Zip Code _____

Education

List the names and addresses of the last four schools you have attended, most recent school first. Include dates.

1. _____   3. _____

   _____   _____

   _____   _____

   Dates _____   Dates _____

2. _____   4. _____

   _____   _____

   _____   _____

   Dates _____   Dates _____

List any skills you have learned in school from classes that you could use on a job.

_____

_____

_____

List any honors or awards you have received.

_____

_____

List any activities (teams, clubs, etc.) in which you have participated. Include any positions of responsibility you have held.

_____

_____

_____

Employment

Informal Jobs:

List any jobs you have done, whether paid or not, for friends or relatives. Include dates.

1. _____

   _____ Date _____

2. _____

   _____ Date _____

3. _____

   _____ Date _____

(continued)

Résumé Information *(continued)*

Formal Work:
List any jobs you have had with regular hours and pay (part- or full-time).
Include the dates you held the jobs and the names and addresses of your
employers.

1. _____

   _____
   Date _____

2. _____

   _____
   Date _____

Personal

List any hobbies or activities you have not already mentioned.

_____

_____

List any long trips you have taken and tell whether they were taken with your
family, a youth group, or alone.

_____

_____

List any skills you have not already mentioned that might be of use to you on a
job.

_____

_____

References

Give the names and addresses of three people who know you well. If possible,
include an employer, someone at your school, and a friend of your family.

1. _____

   _____

2. _____

   _____

3. _____

   _____

Career Goals

Write the job you would like to have after graduation. List any special training or
certificates you will need after high school for the job.

_____

Résumé

STUDY
THIS

John L. Langdon

327 Michigan Avenue
Provo, Utah 84601
(801) 555-9745

Education

1993 to 1996	North High School, Provo, Utah
1990 to 1993	Mason Middle School, Provo, Utah
1984 to 1990	East Hills Elementary School, Prescott, Arizona
School Activities:	Varsity Football Team Block-N Club Vice president of Guitar Club

Employment

June 1996 to Sept. 1996	Santo's Pizzeria 2234 Third Street, Provo, Utah Cook
Sept. 1995 to June 1996	North High School 9883 West Road, Provo, Utah Cafeteria helper
May 1994 to April 1995	Provo *Globe* Provo, Utah Newspaper carrier
June 1994 to August 1994	Did yard chores for neighbors on vacation

Personal

Born: Oakland, California, on May 23, 1979
Marital Status: Single
Health: Excellent

Special Skills: Holder of Utah driver's license
Type 30 words per minute
Speak Spanish

References

Santo Petronni
Santo's Pizzeria
2234 Third Street
Provo, Utah

Catherine Goodly
North High School
9883 West Road
Provo, Utah

James Espinoza
765 Woodlawn Way
Provo, Utah

Career Goals: Associate in Arts degree in restaurant management
Management career in restaurant industry

CHAPTER 16

Abbreviations

Many of the abbreviations presented in this chapter are included in writing competency tests we have examined.

Following the worksheets with abbreviations and their derivatives are three exercises for student practice. The whole business of learning abbreviations is one of memorization.

You can allow time in class for students to practice with a partner. You can also set up activities such as the old-fashioned spelling bee, using abbreviations instead of words, and flash cards with abbreviations on one side and derivatives on the other, if time in the class permits. If not, students can be given the lists of abbreviations and told to memorize them.

The exercises can be used first as exercises, then as tests if needed.

STUDY
THESE

Common Abbreviations

Mr.	Mister
Mrs.	Missis or Missus (originally Mistress)
Ms.	Miss or Mrs.
Dr.	Doctor
St.	Saint or Street
Jr.	Junior
Sr.	Senior
B.A.	Bachelor of Arts
B.S.	Bachelor of Science
Ph.D.	Doctor of Philosophy
M.D.	Doctor of Medicine
D.D.S.	Doctor of Dental Surgery
Rev.	Reverend
Hon.	Honorable
Prof.	Professor
L.P.N.	Licensed Practical Nurse
R.N.	Registered Nurse
Ed.	Editor
Man.	Manager
Pub.	Publisher
A.D.	anno Domini (after Christ was born)
B.C.	before Christ (was born)
A.M.	ante meridiem (morning—after midnight)
P.M.	post meridiem (afternoon and evening)
etc.	and so forth
e.g.	for example
i.e.	that is
et al.	and others
mph	miles per hour
rpm	revolutions per minute
Rd.	Road
Dr.	Drive
Ln.	Lane
Blvd.	Boulevard
Ave.	Avenue
Hwy.	Highway
P.S.	postscript (after a letter)

STUDY THESE

Abbreviations for Measurements

Length

in	inch(es)
ft	foot or feet
yd	yard(s)
mi	mile(s)
mm	millimeter(s)
cm	centimeter(s)
dm	decimeter(s)
m	meter(s)
km	kilometer(s)

Weight

oz	ounce(s)
lb	pound(s)
mg	milligram(s)
g	gram(s)
kg	kilogram(s)

Volume

tsp	teaspoon(s)
tbs	tablespoon(s)
pt	pint(s)
qt	quart(s)
gal	gallon(s)
ml	milliliter(s)
l	liter(s)

Name _____

Date _____

Titles

FILL IT IN

Fill in the correct abbreviation for each of the words below:

1. Mister _____

2. Missis or Missus _____

3. Miss or Mrs. _____

4. Doctor _____

5. Saint _____

6. Junior _____

7. Senior _____

8. Bachelor of Arts _____

9. Bachelor of Science _____

10. Doctor of Philosophy _____

11. Doctor of Medicine _____

12. Doctor of Dental Surgery _____

13. Reverend _____

14. Honorable _____

15. Professor _____

16. Registered Nurse _____

17. Licensed Practical Nurse _____

18. Editor _____

19. Manager _____

20. Publisher _____

Other Abbreviations

FILL IT IN

Fill in the correct abbreviations for the words below:

1. anno Domini

2. before Christ

3. morning hours

4. afternoon hours

5. and so forth

6. for example

7. that is

8. and others

9. miles per hour

10. revolutions per minute

11. Street

12. Road

13. Drive

14. Lane

15. Boulevard

16. Avenue

17. Highway

18. postscript

TRY THIS

Use the abbreviations for words 5 through 8 in sentences.

5. _____

_____

6. _____

_____

7. _____

_____

8. _____

_____

Name _____

Date _____

Measurements

FILL IT IN

Write the abbreviations for the measurements indicated:

1. inch _____
2. foot or feet _____
3. yard _____
4. mile _____
5. millimeter _____
6. centimeter _____
7. decimeter _____
8. meter _____
9. kilometer _____
10. ounce _____
11. pound _____
12. milligram _____
13. gram _____
14. kilogram _____
15. teaspoon _____
16. tablespoon _____
17. pint _____
18. quart _____
19. gallon _____
20. milliliter _____
21. liter _____

TRY THIS

Write the words and abbreviations we have not studied that you know:

_____ _____ _____ _____

_____ _____ _____ _____

_____ _____ _____ _____

_____ _____ _____ _____